Developing Explosive Athletes

Use of Velocity Based Training In Athletes

By

J. Bryan Mann, PhD.

With Foreword By

Kaz Kazadi

Developing Explosive Athletes

Use of Velocity Based Training in Athletes

By
J. Bryan Mann, PhD.

Foreword by
Kaz Kazadi

Published by:
Ultimate Athlete Concepts
Michigan, USA
2021
For information or to order copies: www.uaconcepts.com

Mann, J. Bryan.
Developing Explosive Athletes
Includes Bibliographical References.
ISBN: 978-1540558824

ISBN: 1540558827

Edited by Steve Gunn

Printed in the United States of America

Published by Ultimate Athlete Concepts

Website: www.uaconcepts.com

Table of Contents

Foreword

Whether it's Walter Payton exploding to dive over the pile on the way into the end zone, Usain Bolt confidently obliterating world records in the Olympic games, or Michael Jordan effortlessly planting his signature Air Jordans behind the free throw line and soaring to the rim for a mind- blowing throw down, the sporting world has long had a love affair with amazing feats of speed and power. This passion has fully engulfed the sporting world, making quotes such as "speed kills" part of the every day vernacular of coaches everywhere. The pursuit of power has reached such a mythical stature that it is believed by many in the athletic universe that improving power production is the "end all be all."

Unfortunately, there are many coaches, athletes and trainers who still hold on to the belief that speed and power can't be taught. However, it can be trained. Therefore, it is fair to say that the star athletes named above had genetic predispositions that allowed them to reach the pinnacle of achievement in their sports. It must also be recognized that it was only through a combination of genetics and training that these athletes reached their highest potential.

For a coach, training for power can often be an extremely frustrating endeavor. After all, locomotive speed can be easily quantified by time, and strength efforts are simply measured by the amount of weight moved. But how can we quantify power production as displayed in the weight room? Clearly, we know that two athletes moving the same amount of weight are not necessarily producing the same amount of power. Now, with the advent of specialized equipment like the Tendo unit, Gymaware, Eliteform and many others, coaches are able to measure the speed at which an object is moving, and adjust training to ensure the optimal training effect.

But what is optimal? What does it mean when one athlete moves an object faster than another athlete? How can we adjust the training of these athletes to ensure that they both benefit from their training? These, along with other considerations and uses for velocity-based training (VBT), demand the in-depth discussion provided by Bryan Mann in the following pages.

From the moment Bryan and I were introduced to each other as graduate assistants at the University of Missouri, he has remained one of my most valuable advisors in the field of performance training. I immediately developed a tremendous amount of respect and appreciation for his unwavering hunger for knowledge. From one-on-one tutoring sessions that have proven immensely beneficial for my professional development to arguments and discussions about effective and ineffective training methods, our conversations have always been passionate and enthusiastic. Looking back on our mutual experience of long days and sleepless nights under the rule of Pat Ivey, it only makes sense that I was asked to write this foreword for Bryan, as few other people could have an appreciation for his unrelenting pursuit of athletically pertinent training methods.

A few months ago, I received a call from Bryan, who excitedly told me that he would soon be involved in a roundtable symposium at the 2008 Collegiate Strength and Conditioning Coaches National Conference, discussing the uses and benefits of the Tendo unit. He asked me what I thought about the great news, and I replied, "Man, Mann, an hour ain't long enough. You're gonna have to write a book."

Kaz Kazadi
Assistant Athletic Director for Athletic Performance
Baylor University

Prologue

In this third edition, I have found out the answers to many previously unknown topics. There are also some explanations to answers that I had (i.e. I knew what happened but not why). I hope this edition answers as much for you as it has for me.

My journey with velocity-based training (VBT) started without a device at all. In 1999, I started working for a man named Rick Perry, who, at the time of this writing, is an assistant strength and conditioning coach for the Chicago Bears. Rick had what seemed like a quite extensive library of translated Soviet texts on training, by authors such as Verkhoshansky, Roman and Medvedev. He encouraged me, as a young undergraduate, to read all of these books. In some of these Soviet texts, I kept seeing this strange "m/s" denotation. I didn't have any idea what it was, but thought it might be useful one day. In 2001, Rick brought me with him to visit Louie Simmons of Westside Barbell fame. Louie had just written an article on this thing called the Tendo and, at the time, it was the only device that measured velocity. We got a Tendo, and we started applying what Louie had said and what I had read in the old Soviet manuals. What ensued was fantastic. We could tell if an athlete was moving an appropriate load or if an athlete was going too light or too heavy, all in a matter of seconds.

My experience with velocity increased when I was at the University of Missouri with Pat Ivey. Much to our surprise, the results of a statistics project showed that we didn't have any relationship between our Olympic lifts and improvements in the vertical jump. We got a Tendo and tested our guys. While the literature said we should be moving the bar at over 1.3 meters/second (m/s) average velocity, our guys were moving it at around 0.6 m/s. Obviously, it was way off. After using the velocities to dictate the load on cleans for awhile, we found that there was a relationship between the two. Overall, we saw improvements in transfer of training with everything we used velocity on.

Next, various devices that measure velocity became available, and the innovations and advancement were amazing. Now, with products like GymAware, we can get around 15 times the amount of information that we could with the Tendo. Beyond GymAware, there are a multitude of devices that measure or calculate velocity.

I was at a conference and someone came up to me and said, "What the hell are you going to start calling the stuff you do now, because Tendo is no longer the only show in town?" I looked at him and said, "Hell if I know. Velocity-based training?" It stuck. At one point, I felt that everyone needed to use velocity and everything needed to be done by velocity. I have since changed my thinking. I think velocity is nice. It definitely improves performance and gives the athlete and the practitioner a lot of information, but it isn't for everyone. Nothing is wrong with percentage-based training. It works and it works well. In fact, the traits that we utilize for velocity work

Figure 1. The king of exercises being done with velocity.

perfectly with Bosco's strength continuum that he first published in the mid-80s. Velocity really works as a compliment to this and aids in the exactness of work.

I have come to explain it like this: Percentage-based training is like a map. If I go outside and I have a map, I can do a really good job of figuring out how to get to where I want to go if I can figure out what surrounds me and where those things are on the map. If I look at the map and make various twists and turns when it looks like I'm supposed to, I will successfully end up at my destination. Velocity-based training is like GPS. If I go outside with my GPS, I know exactly where I am at every moment. I know exactly how many feet until my next turn and exactly when I will reach my destination. Some people like maps and some people like GPS. You have your choice of what to use.

Introduction

Velocity-based training (VBT) is an excellent tool for coaches or strength and conditioning professionals. It uses bar speed, allowing a lifter to train exactly where he needs to for that specific lift on that particular day. It can replace the use of percentage-based training, allowing for maximal results, and helps coaches utilize the training method known as autoregulation.

"Autoregulatory" refers to a volume management system used to regulate individual differences in work capacity, and allows these differences to be self-governed and applied. In other words, the coach allows the athlete to progress at his own rate (J. B. Mann, Thyfault, Ivey, & Sayers, 2010).

Every athlete has his own rate of progress. Coaches do not want to impede an individual athlete's progress because of a more slowly developing athlete. They also don't want the more slowly developing athlete to push his development to that of the more quickly developing athlete, which would result in either overtraining or injury. Overtraining would negate all of the gains made in the program, and injury would prevent the athlete from being able to compete.

Autoregulation also helps to take into account other stressors. In Selye's book, *The Stress of Life*, he states that all stressors draw from the same pool. So when training athletes, all stressors in their lives must be accounted for, including practice, game play, weight training, conditioning, speed development, education, relationship issues, family issues, night life and other factors. If coaches do not account for these, their program may not be optimized.

Important note: When this text was originally written, the only means of measuring velocity was the linear position transducer. Now, there are several means of measuring velocity, including the linear position transducer (LPT), barbell accelorometers, body accelerometers, time motion analysis and 3D camera-based capture, among others. These different tools all measure velocity a bit differently. Some units have a great agreement with LPT and some do not. If the research shows that they have a great relationship with LPT, by all means utilize the information in this book. If they do not, it may be necessary to collect a velocity profile and go from there with the same concepts. If they do produce different measurements, that does not necessarily mean that they are wrong. They are just measuring from a different means. As long as it's consistent, it's fine to use.

Now how is it different but still accurate? Well, let's stop and take a different view on it. I have gotten into woodworking as of late as a hobby. I have several different tape measures. Each measures the wood slightly differently, due to play in the clip or some other reason. This makes it tough if I measure the area of the project with one tape measure but measure the wood to be cut with a different tape measure. The project may be slightly too big or too small to fit in the area.

But if I use the same tape measure to measure the project area and cut the wood, everything is perfect. The same concepts apply to the different velocity measurements. If you measure one day on a body accelerometer and the next day on a linear position transducer, you will wind up with problems. However, if you pick one device and stick with it, the reliability of the device will allow you to have similar outcomes. The velocity zones and bands may vary, but overall it will be similar.

Load-Velocity Profile

Some of you may be asking what a velocity profile is, while others may already know. Lately (starting in 2014 and 2015), many coaches and companies have been talking about developing a velocity profile. Some speak very vaguely of it, as if it is something very mystical. It is not mystical at all. Briefly, let's discuss what it is, how you find it and how you use it.

What it is

The velocity profile is simply the velocities that you move for various percentages of a one-rep max (RM). It has been found that while strength may vary, the corresponding velocities at percentages of a 1RM do not. A 2009 study by Jidovtseff found that velocity and corresponding percentages of a 1RM were very strong, not only for the individual but for the group on the bench press. Jidovtseff actually developed an equation to predict velocity from the desired percentage of a 1RM (Jidovtseff, Quièvre, Hanon, & Crielaard, 2009). Another study found the same relationship when using a pre/post-test design. Gonzalez-Badillo (González-Badillo & Sánchez-Medina, 2010) found that there was, on average, a 0.00–0.01 meters/second (m/s) variation between the two, although the group did increase its max an average of 9.6 percent . This demonstrated the near perfect relationship that existed between percentages of a 1RM and the corresponding velocity. It did not matter what the strength change was. The velocity at the corresponding percentage was exactly the same.

There have been multiple methods of doing this, such as the one prescribed above. Recent research has been attempting to develop more parsimonious means of doing velocity profiling. One such study comes from _____ et al. In this study, they attempted to use a 2-load method for profiling the athlete. They found that by taking the best repetition at 20% of 1RM, and the best repetition at 80% of 1RM, they found the same information as they would collecting the entire range within the profile. This does enable the practitioner to quickly profile the athlete for monitoring purposes. Two repetitions is an attainable volume that would not slow down or negatively impact training, and as such would appear to be sustainable.

While this is obviously a parsimonious method requiring little data collection, it is not without its flaws. For instance, would it actually be practical and safe to jump from 20 to 80 percent of 1RM? When working with the University of Missouri football team from 2004-2016, most of our offensive and defensive linemen were on the average 600-pound squatters, ranging from 365-800 pounds. For the athletes with a 365 max, this would be a repetition at 73 pounds and a repetition at 292 pounds. For the majority of athletes who squatted around 600 pounds, this would be a repetition at 120 pounds and 480 pounds. For the few athletes who were in the 800 pound range, this would be a repetition at 160 pounds and a repetition at 640 pounds.

For the athletes who were squatting only 365, it's a bit on the crazy side to make jumps of that size, but it's not uncommon for athletes to attempt to do their first sets at 275l-315 pounds without much warmup. This is not safe, but it is often noticed that they attempt to do this in the quest to save time. For athletes squatting 600 or 800 pounds, it is absolutely insane to make these sorts of jumps. This is a 360- or 480-pound increase! There's an old saying - "Just because you can doesn't mean you should." Yes, it is completely possible to do the two-load method, and it is mathematically accurate. But a 480-pound jump would be too much for the nervous system to adapt to, let alone the musculoskeletal system.

One thing that may increase the efficiency yet decrease the accuracy of velocity profiling may be the use of mass cutoffs. When utilizing a single velocity cutoff, it allows the practitioner to run one single model for the prediction to gain the information with each athlete. This does have some flaws, of course. Some athletes may be achieving their 1RM at .3m/s, some at .25, and in extreme cases up over .4m/s. This obviously demonstrates that there would be differences in 1RM velocities for the athletes. However, I liken this method to what I call bathroom scale theory. It does not matter if my bathroom scale reads inline with the scale in the doctor's office or not, because it reads the same way every day. It will let me know if I am gaining or losing weight, regardless of what the actual number is and how it has a discrepancy from the doctor's' office. Much like this, if you're just looking to follow the athlete over the course of time, this is a good enough method. You see the direction that the athlete is going – is he or she getting stronger, maintaining their current level, or decreasing in strength? You can then alter your training means to match what is happening and what you're attempting to do.

 Is their strength decreasing while you are in-season? Maybe your attempt has been to go with submaximal intensities and higher volumes and they are overtraining. A possible fix for this would be to increase the intensity and decrease the volume. The converse is also true. If you are going with high intensities and low volumes and the athlete is showing a decrease in strength, lower the intensity and increase the volume.

How you find it

Whenever you test for a RM (the lower the better; I prefer a 1RM myself), you record the velocities that were taken at each percentage of the 1RM. You have recorded what velocity you moved at with each corresponding weight.

How you use it

Once you know your velocity profile, you can simply assign the velocities that you would move at a certain percentage, rather than the percentage itself. For instance, if I move 60 percent at about 0.8 m/s, any time I had 60 percent, I would assign 0.8 m/s for the loading intensity, rather than the 60 percent. Also, it can utilize the daily slope along with a terminal velocity to assign the percentages of a 1RM. Understanding this relationship and how it varies by exercise increases the likelihood that you will correctly select the load. It will also give you one more metric to use to watch for trends with your athletes.

The following table (table 1) is from my personal workouts on the bench press. As you can see, on Aug. 22, 2015, my estimated 1RM was 396 pounds, and my peak mean force occurred at 225 pounds. This was six days before the birth of my daughter. It may be interesting for some to see that the alteration of velocity on my final set at 365 pounds was actually faster than my velocity at 345 pounds. Many may find that peculiar. On this given day, I actually tried to mentally prepare myself or psych myself up for 365 pounds. With 345 pounds, I simply lay down and did it.

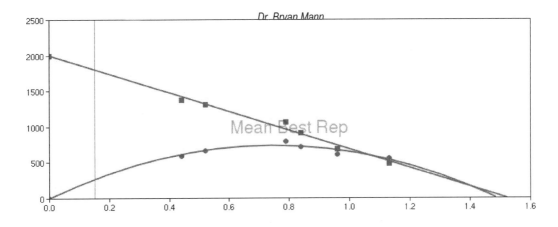

Figure 2. Velocity profile for bench press on Aug. 22, 2015.

Table 1. The accompanying loads, mean velocities, powers and forces to make up the previous velocity profile.			
Bench press **Predicted 1RM,** **Bryan Mann, Aug. 22, 2015, 396.1 lbs, 0.15 m/s**			
Weight	Mean velocity (m/s)	Mean power (W)	Mean force (N)
45.0 lbs	1.21	308.75	244.11
95.0 lbs	0.93	429.72	482.49
135.0 lbs	1.04	698.53	691.24
185.0 lbs	0.8	670.06	878.65
225.0 lbs	0.73	746.23	1076.67
275.0 lbs	0.5	619.13	1268.17
315.0 lbs	0.42	590.81	1438.19
345.0 lbs	0.23	351.47	1531.91
365.0 lbs	0.3	489.35	1622.32

If we look at the following chart (table 2), we see my first "real" workout after my daughter's birth. I had been doing some training, at least whatever I could muster. However, for those who have children, you know that isn't a whole heck of a lot. I was in a sleep-deprived state and got caffeinated to the gills to have a good training session. You can see that my estimated 1RM this day was only 335 pounds, a full 61 pounds lower than my previous training session. Around eight weeks had gone by, and my max had dropped off 61 pounds. We all know how stress affects the body and that it is systemic. The stress of having a new baby, a lack of sleep and a changing family environment had taken its toll on me. If I had actually attempted a 1RM on this day, it is quite likely that I would have been injured.

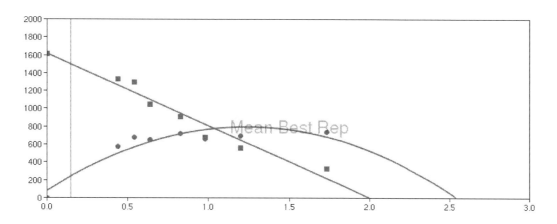

Figure 3. Velocity profile for a bench press on Oct. 17, 2015.

Table 2. The weights, velocities, power and forces from Oct. 17, 2015, to make the previous chart.			
Bench press **Predicted 1RM** **Bryan Mann, Oct. 17, 2015, 335.7 lbs, 0.15 m/s**			
Weight	**Mean Velocity (m/s)**	**Mean Power (W)**	**Mean Force (N)**
45.0 lb	1.73	739.29	328.4
95.0 lb	1.2	691.4	560.56
135.0 lb	0.98	662.71	681.75
185.0 lb	0.83	721.18	910.11
225.0 lb	0.64	651.34	1050.86
275.0 lb	0.54	674.17	1295.64
290.0 lb	0.44	571.84	1326.95

Assumptions of the load-velocity profile

The velocity profile does have two possibly fatal flaws. It assumes that the device you are using is reliable. Unfortunately, some units go to market, even though they are unreliable, because of the company trying to make a profit. The other assumption that is made is that the athlete moved as fast as possible to complete the concentric portion of the movement.

Downsides of the load-velocity profile

The downsides of the velocity profile occur when you are using large groups. Having worked with groups of up to 100 athletes at a time when dealing with track and field, it was imperative to find a way to do things quickly and easily. If you could tell the entire team to stay between one velocity and a second, you are more apt to get them to do what is desired by the coach. If 100 people have 100 different velocities, you start to run into problems. This is where the zones came into effect. We knew and understood that if we had to get everyone on the same page, it may not be perfect, but it would probably still be effective.

Another downside to the velocity profile is that, as one continues to get stronger and trains in heavier loads, they experience adaptations of this. The body adapts to be able to continue to strain through slower and slower velocities without failing, and this is called neuromuscular efficiency (Helms et al., 2017). For instance, it is typical for team sport athletes to achieve 1Rm at 0.3m/s on a squat, it is typical for a powerlifter to achieve 1Rm at approximately 0.15m/s, and not uncommon to see lifters be able to still complete the lift at 0.08m/s. Additionally, there is something called a Force-Velocity-Power profile that we will address later in the text. This is essentially a means of using VBT as an assessment to understand how the athlete produces power and how prescriptions may be altered to maximize the athletes' abilities.

Some research has shown that strength-speed was best developed at 0.75 m/s for a bench press and 1.0 m/s for a squat, and the percentages were close on each. Some practitioners who deal with smaller teams have utilized individual

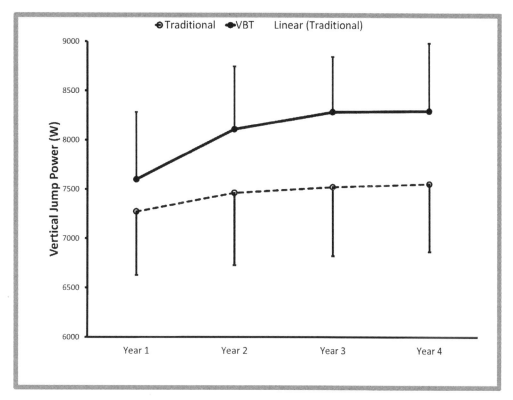

Figure 4. This chart represents four years of pre-season training for Division I athletes. Those utilizing VBT showed much greater gains in power than those who did not.

velocity profiles with great success. I like the zones because of their applicability to such a wide range of athletes on a wide range of lifts in a wide range of sports, and they have worked for nearly all of them.

We have read several papers, such as the one from Jacobson and colleagues (Bert H. Jacobson, Conchola, Glass, & Thompson, 2013), that say college football players tend to gain power during the first year as they gain strength, but not after this. As you can see by this chart (figure 4) from a poster presentation at the 2016 NSCA, the utilization of velocity zones allowed the team to continue to gain power far beyond this.

As you can see from the figure above (figure 4), the use of VBT allowed the athletes to continue to gain power through the third year. There was a leveling off at year four. We theorized that if we were to move to developing speed-strength on the squat and a faster Olympic lift such as the snatch, the trend may continue into a fourth year and beyond. However, as is often the case in strength and conditioning, there was a staff turnover, so this theory will never be tested, at least not for many years, if ever.

In deeper examination since the previous edition, my views have evolved slightly on this. By looking at our results in this case of a multiyear program, it is evident that the implementation of VBT bought us approximately two years of development on the athlete. However, there was a clear point in which the VBT no longer transferred to the sport.

If we refer back to Bondarchuk's classifications of exercise, we remember that there were four - GPE, SPE, SDE and CE. GPE, or General Preparatory exercise, is the general exercise classification that is essentially training muscles and joints of the body in a general way, which may or may not involve those in the sport and are not regarded for their planar involvements. SPE, or Special Preparatory exercise, increases specificity and transfer to the exercises, which usually increases in specificity down to the joints involved and the planes of movement that are involved. SDE, or Special Developmental Exercise, increases specificity because you are recreating a portion of the competitive exercise to derive the greatest transfer. The competitive exercise varies by how this is done, but can be the event or sport itself, or something that's a component of that sport.

For the hammer throw, which is Dr. Bondarchuk's background, this would simply be throwing the competition weight hammer.

While squats would be considered a GPE exercise, I think that by adding in velocity we are enhacing the neural capability through improvement and rate coding, increasing the transfer of the squat and essentially making it a SPE category. Viewing the work of Vherkoshansky and Yessis, we see that the general exercises will transfer for a while to the event. We also see in a another text the diminishing returns of strength occuring at a 2.2x's bodyweight strength level (Suchomel, Nimphius, & Stone, 2016). However the transfer is very limited, and once the requisite level of strength in the general exercise is achieved, further enhancement of those capabilities will not lead to any increase in sports performance.

These theories are confirmed in studies by Jacobson and Miller separately, as well as our own data presented here and at the 2016 NSCA National Meeting. By enhancing the GPE exercise to an SPE exercise, we increased the utility of the exercise by two years, but there was an obvious ceiling.

During this time period, strength-speed was the only trait that was used for power development on the squat, and the hang power clean was the only barbell exercise that was done for speed-strength. Theoretically, we may have seen another incremental increase for power enhancement if we utilized bands on the squats and performed them for speed-strength, and changed from the hang power clean to the hang power snatch. It is completely possible, however, that our ability to adapt and enhance performance through SPE means we would not have seen another increase from this category of exercise. At this point we may have needed to utilize SDE categorization of exercises to further stimulate increases. I do believe that there are alterations of GPE that can make something SDE for certain actions. Rhea et al, in their 2016 paper, demonstrated how the ½ and ¼ squat transferred better to the sprints and jumps than full squats (note - this did not state, nor did the study state, that full squats did not transfer, only that there were greater increases in sprint speed and jumping ability as a result of the former two exercises to the latter). This again is consistent with work tjhat came out of the former Soviet Union by Vherkoshansky and Bondarchuk, among others, and brought to the USA by Yessis. There are also exercises not related to the GPE exercises that may show great transfer, depending on the sport or event, such as the knee drive, paw back, hip shift, and several others.

I will never know what the impact of the change from the clean to a snatch, the change from strength-speed to speed-strength, or the implementation of SDE would have on this population. In college athletics, like the real world, the only true constant is change, and we underwent a staffing change that prevented us from being able to implement this strategy.

The upside to utilizing velocity profiles is that you know exactly what velocity the athlete should be using for the desired trait. When you are dealing with individuals or small groups of very intelligent athletes, this is the most precise way to do it. That being said, a small diversion to a story about Dr. Andy Fry is warranted. Dr. Fry once said, "You know, as researchers, we get very worried and concerned about precision. Is this exact enough? Are there any other possibilities here? Do we have everything explained to a T? With the coaches, you have to work with large groups and it has to be workable and implementable. For coaches, it's not about precision. It's about real world results and being good enough. If you get too precise, it may not work for the practitioner."

What VBT Does

Simply put, velocity-based training (VBT) uses bar speed. By knowing the speed of the lift and/or strength, the coach can adjust the weight on the bar. Louie Simmons first introduced the Tendo FitroDyne to most people in the United States in a *Powerlifting USA* article (Simmons, 2002).

With every repetition completed, the athlete knows immediately after completing the repetition whether or not he had a good repetition. Think about feedback, what it has done for the education process, and how it allows for refinement of skill. Through the

Figure 5. Using feedback to dial in the appropriate load on a snatch.

works of Dr. Gabriele Wulf (Wulf, 2007), we know that external focus is a way to increase performance. If you are already giving external cues, such as push the ground away, push the bar away or blast off like a rocket, you are getting a lot of bang for your buck. On top of the technique cue, we now get an external cue and feedback about the speed of the repetition. This makes the intention of the movement clear and often allows the athlete to see a much greater result in his performance as a consequence of his more focused attention.

Another way to think about this goes back to a writing composition class. Many people who have had these sorts of classes wrote a multitude of papers. You write a paper, receive it back from the professor filled with red marks, and improve on the next paper. Each and every paper hopefully improves as you take the feedback of the instructor and try to improve your work, each and every time.

The measurement of speed is purely objective. It doesn't see the athletes, and it doesn't know who they are. It's completely objective. Many times during an explosive exercise I've told athletes that they were moving too slowly and that they needed to perform the movement faster. They've looked at me like I'm crazy and responded with, "Coach, you must be on crack because that was blazing fast." The velocity reading gives them objective feedback. If they're supposed to be moving at 1.0 meters/second (m/s) and they're only at 0.75 m/s, they obviously aren't moving fast enough because the reading shows them the actual speed. So athletes who previously gave you looks like you were crazy and told you that you were wrong will now say, "Coach, I'm not moving fast enough. I have to pick it up."

The use of velocity also elicits the competitive nature of the athlete. Quite often, two athletes will be using the same weight for an exercise. One athlete will move the weight faster than the other, and they will both start talking back and forth and getting competitive. Soon it will become the greatest explosive strength workout that they've ever had because they don't want to be beaten. Athletes are often cocky and flamboyant. VBT is a good way to nurture this competitive spirit and help them become better athletes. In turn, it will also improve their workouts.

A 2011 study by Randell and colleagues looked at the effect that feedback of peak velocity had on performance of sports specific tasks (Randell, Cronin, Keogh, Gill, & Pedersen, 2011). They took rugby players and divided them into two groups. One group had no feedback while the other group did have feedback. They performed the exact same workout with the exact same loads. The group that was provided the feedback saw greater increases in sprinting ability and jumping ability than the non-feedback group. Athletes want to know how they are doing, if they are meeting their goals and if they are doing things properly. Using velocity gives the coach one more tool to let the athletes know how they are doing. With the feedback, the athletes are able to obtain a higher quality of work, which impacted them with greater gains in speed and explosive power.

One key issue that needs to be addressed is accuracy. I've been asked over and over, "How do I know the velocity is accurate?" Many people think that high speed cameras are needed to determine the velocity of the bar, but this isn't so. A study done by Jennings and colleagues found that the FitroDyne was in fact a reliable and valid way to measure power generated during

Figure 6. Utilizing velocity as feedback on a squat jump to improve power.

a weightlifting movement (Jennings, Viljoen, Durandt, & Lambert, 2005). There have been other studies using other linear position transducers as a means of calculating velocity for many years. In fact, the linear position transducer is still considered the gold standard for velocity measurements in research for weightlifting type exercises.

Let's take an imaginary and extreme example, yet one that isn't at all uncommon, that many coaches have encountered. Johnny is a football player who is on the borderline of academic ineligibility and must get at least a B on his history midterm to maintain eligibility. He has been studying from 10:00 a.m. until 10:30 p.m. when his girlfriend calls him. They have been dating for six months, and the conversation goes something like this: "Johnny, I don't love you anymore. I've never loved you. I don't want to see you again so don't call me! Bye!"

After a few choice words, Johnny is completely devastated. He calls his friends, and they do what any good college friend would do in a situation like this — they take him out and get him drunk. So Johnny is drinking Jack Daniels until 2:30 a.m. and then goes to bed. The alarm clock starts ringing, and Johnny makes it in to his 6:00 a.m. lifting group where he is scheduled to hit 92 percent for three sets of two reps. With all the stressors currently acting upon Johnny's body, this 92 percent is no longer 92 percent. It's more like 107 percent, and trying to complete the workout may get Johnny hurt.

This is an extreme example, but it is one that illustrates the point quite well. Everything acts on the body, and a good coach will try and account for that as best he can. VBT is fantastic for picking up on these factors as well because velocity is the first thing to go, as found by Fry and colleagues in a recent presentation given at the University of Missouri Strength and Conditioning clinic. Power will decrease first, and greatly so with overtraining. Sprints and agility greatly decrease as well. Oddly enough, maximal strength holds on for a while.

The theory presented by Fry and colleagues is that an athlete can simply force himself to grind things out slowly and achieve the same weights (Fry et al., 1994). While he could still continue to make gains in absolute strength for a short while, his power has deteriorated. When he is able to examine and identify exactly when his power declines, the volume and intensity can be reduced, which could possibly prevent overtraining.

One admission about the use of VBT is that athletes can cheat the system. If athletes don't want to work hard, they can move the bar more slowly on purpose and thus end up with a lighter weight.

One way to get around this is to limit the use of VBT to only those athletes who have established a high level of trust and are in higher levels of the program. The University of Missouri football team uses a multi-leveled program, which is based on several factors, including absolute strength numbers, hypertrophy needs, explosive strength, comparison to standards and, most importantly, the trust of the coaches. It is not based on playing time or related factors.

Figure 7. Utilizing velocity on a trap bar deadlift to determine appropriate loads for the desired trait for that given day.

The football team at Missouri established a system where athletes work hard because they want to improve their athletic performance and achieve those higher levels. They don't get to use VBT until they have reached the level where they have earned the coaches' trust.

4 pillars of force production enhancement

Before we proceed any further, I want to present to you something that is common sense, but is often lost in today's talk of advanced training models. While many talk in modes of sensationalism, I think we need to stop and think about common sense. There are four main areas in which the muscle can enhance force production. If the training doesn't fit into one of these four categories (except for enhancement of the parallel elastic component), it is probably sensationalizing and won't really work.

Myofibrilar adaptations: Through traditional resistance training, the myofibril itself
is often targeted. The increase in the size of the heavy chain myosin will
increase the force capabilities of the muscle directly, and through the
increase in diameter, will change the angle of pennation, which is how the
muscle comes into the tendon. By becoming more and more oblique
toward perpendicular, more of the applied force goes toward a rotary force
and torque, making a more efficient line of pull to cause rotation of the
lever and thus movement. In addition to this, the ability of the myosin head
to hold on to the actin filament improves, which increases the ability of the
muscle to withstand force before the myosin head breaks apart (as well as
the deformation of the myosin neck and the actin as it is connected to the
next actin by the titin). To increase the myofibrillar adaptations, loads of 6-
12RM should be lifted for 2-6 sets unless utilizing plyometrics. If trying to

directly improve the withstanding of force, accentuated eccentrics should be used.

Sarcoplasmic reticulum: The sarcoplasmic reticulum is an indirect force enhancer. It is in charge of the release and reabsorption of calcium, which allows for the polarization to move the troponin away from the tropomyosin to reveal an active binding site. Enhancing the sarcoplasmic reticulum's function increases the speed of which the calcium is released and reabsorbed, speeding up the process of the twitches for the contraction of the muscle to keep up with the rate at which the action potentials reach the muscle. The best way to enhance this is through sprinting.

Hennemen's size principle: This is the principle which governs the recruitment of muscle fibers. Essentially, the high threshold motor units which have the greatest force production potential are not utilized in normal voluntary contractions. It is almost like there is a gate around them to keep them from being called upon as a protective mechanism. When the athlete has been trained with maximal intensity, the body learns how to open this gate and do so with lower and lower necessary action potentials, which can enhance speed and power as it presents on the field.

Rate coding: This is the rate at which the nervous system delivers action potential down the motor neuron to the muscle fiber/cell. When the training is more toward the velocity end of the spectrum, rate coding tends to improve and allow for more synchronous contractions, which enhance the force at high velocities. A recent paper by Pareja-Blanco et al demonstrated that this is where the primary advantages of VBT lie, in the development of rate coding.

Our cognitive biases

One more area to address before we enter into the methodology is a discussion of our biases.

Most people have entered the field of S&C for a love of the weight room. This has often translated into entering into the sports of powerlifting and Olympic weightlifting. What's interesting to me at this point in my career is the clear biases toward maximal lifts within these two sports, in the thought that it would make our athletes better. I know that I for one had that.

Here is an example of my own growth, looking back over the course of my career. I admit to knowing all along that I'm a bit of contrarian, and unless I was told why I shouldn't, I would find a way to do something (and do it well) if I heard it couldn't be done. When I was starting in the field, everyone said "you have to do Olympic lifts, that's the only way to get more explosive." As a powerlifter, I did not like hearing this. I thought my sport was the best sport out there, and that by focusing on my sport rather than theirs, I could do just as good a job, if not better than they did. I focused on strength, did some dynamic effort, and saw fantastic results. We got stronger, we got faster, and we were able to do better on the field.

Through my endeavors in powerlifting, I came across Louie Simmons, who had written an article on the Tendo. I happened to go to Westside Barbell with my first boss Rick Perry shortly after Louie got the Tendo in, and having read much of the translated Soviet texts, I knew what to do with the device. We continued to focus on strength-speed and speed-strength, which we thought were the same at the time and only a translation issue. At some point we started to understand that they weren't the same thing - they were two different sides of the same coin of power. I started doing squats with heavy band tension to get to over 1m/s and hit the speed-strength trait, but wanted more variation.

My contrarian side surfaced once again on my venture to Westside Barbell, then I was out drinking with some friends I had met there. They were talking about how stupid Olympic lifts were, and how there was no place for them. Out of my mouth came the words, "I wouldn't say they're stupid, they're just another means of developing for speed-strength. You can do it through squatting or jumping, you can do it from cleaning or pulling." It seemed like heresy for me to say this as a powerlifter. It may have been the booze talking, but I've often heard that if something still seems like a good idea when the hangover wears off, then it's worth following up on. Well, the hangover wore off, and it still seemed like a good way to look at things.

Later, I had another epiphany when looking at our data gathered over the course of several years. Strength in the main lifts we did stopped transferring to jumps and speed. Many people make the argument that "If you are gaining 30 or 40 pounds and maintaining your speed you're putting out more force." Well, this is as obvious as F=ma. Here is the issue, though. During the first year, when we saw the greatest increases in body mass, we also saw the greatest improvement in speed and power. In the later stages of the athletes' development, there was very little to no gain in muscle mass and also little to no gain in speed and power. Does this mean we need to stimulate hypertrophy? I didn't think so, because I knew many bodybuilders who were far slower as they got bigger. What it signified to me was that we needed to look at other exercises.

I tell this long, drawn out story to illustrate the point that I wasn't looking at speed and power as the main outcomes of training. I was looking at the improvements in the weight room numbers and hoping they transferred to the sprints and the jumps. When they didn't, I ignored it and kept going, because this was what I understood to be true. In the past, some very smart people believed the earth to be the center of the universe, and thought it was flat, as well. Of course both have been proven untrue. I thought I knew that squats were the cure to all athleticism, but now I find that to be untrue. As I have referenced several times now, we have seen from Yessis, Bondarchuk, and Vherkoshansky (among others) that general means transfer to the event or sport for a while. There comes a time, however, when increases in the general means no longer influence performance, and we need to make sure that we shift the emphasis away from that. This is not to say that the goal is to get weaker in these general exercises - that could not be further from the truth. They should still be present, just in a lower proportion, with less time and energy spent on them. After they no longer transfer, they should only take up approximately 20 percent of the time and energy spent on the program.

Where does VBT fit in, anyway?

I have noticed that some trainers have started athletes with VBT, which may not be a good idea. I have had the good fortune to get to know Anatoliy Bondarchuk a fair bit. One thing he said that has really stuck with me is that there is a proper order of training for adaptations to occur. If you go out of order, you lose the adaptation twice. You lose it the first time because the person wasn't ready for it, as they didn't possess the requisite abilities to fully train in the manner required for that method. You will lose it the second time, because you won't see as large of an increase in performance, due to the fact that this stimulus has already been adapted to.

In reverence to Al Vermeil, I have developed something similar to what he calls his performance pyramid. I have my own, because I feel it is important to know and understand what needs to be done to have the best adaptation. This adaptation can be seen in figure (8).

At the base of the pyramid is mobility and work capacity. If the individual is unable to achieve the positions due to a lack of mobility, he or she will not fully benefit from the training. The athlete will also be at a greater risk of injury due to the inability to take the joint through the range of motion without compensating with additional ROM coming from other joints. For instance, if someone is squatting and is required to achieve full depth on the squat, and he has femoral acetabular impingement syndrome (FAI), his femur is going to reach a point where it is unable to increase the angle due to the two femoral neck meeting the acetabulum or labrum, or one bony growth meeting another bony growth. To continue to achieve depth, the individual has no other option but to posteriorly tilt the pelvis to buy additional room within the acetabulum, in order to go around the femoral head and neck so that the appropriate angle can be achieved. Posterior pelvic tilt is always accompanied by lumbar flexion. Lumbar flexion is actually a mechanism for a disc herniation, and when it is done underload it leads to one more risk factor. In essence, by not having mobility to the joint first, by performing multiple repetitions and increasing load, you are making the individual more susceptible to a joint injury.

The next level is base strength. Base strength is developed with intensities around 70 to 85 percent of 1RM. This is what most typically causes the increase in the thickness of the heavy chain myosin isoforms. As this increases in cross sectional area, it increases the amount of force it can withstand and produce. Typically an increase in the other parts of the muscle cell, such as the titin, will increase their abilities to withstand forces, as well. If there isn't sufficient thickness of the heavy chain myosin, the ability to produce power will be subpar and the levels of force will not be sufficient to develop subsequent methods.

Additionally, by increasing the cross sectional area of the muscle fiber, you will also change the angle with which it intersects the tendon, also known as the pennation angle. When the pennation angle is increased, it often will allow more of the force generated to go toward rotation rather than compression or distraction. While those of course are important forces for joint stabilization, they do not allow for enhanced movement.

The next level is absolute strength. Absolute strength is developed when dealing with loads 90 percent and greater. This loading encourages Henneman's size principle, which basically states that the larger motor units require a higher action potential to be sent down the motor neuron. When these are utilized often, they may remap and organize in such a manner that there are fewer sets of motor units in a "circuit" to be able to elicit the contraction of the higher threshold large motor units. This may allow reduced energy to reach the appropriate action potential to engage these motor units. If Henneman's size principle is not fully utilized, and the alternative circuits are not engaged, the high threshold motor units that need to be called upon to deliver maximal performance will not be utilized appropriately.

The next level involves specific strengths, and this is where we often look at strength traits such as strength-speed and speed-strength. When this is utilized it essentially enhances the speed at which the signal, or action potential, is sent down the motor neuron pathway. This is at the end because if you don't have enough force capability in reserve, through the use of larger muscle fibers and high threshold motor units, there is no way to progressively overload these in a manner to elicit further adaptation.

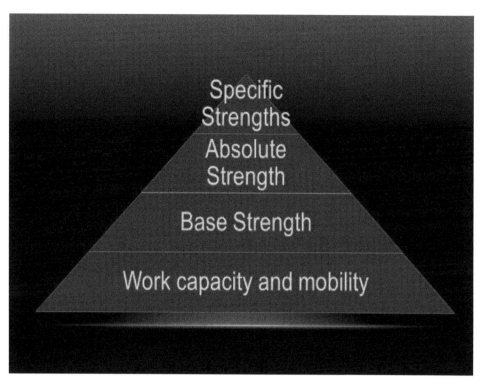

Figure 8 1

Self Determination Theory

There has long been a belief that "a well-coached program will beat a well-written program any day of the week." Those who have been around for a while understand the truth to it. If the athletes are bought into the plan and the personality of the coach, they will work because they want to work. This falls into line with intrinsic motivation. Within the realm of internisic motivation, there is Deci & Ryan's Self-Determination Theory (SDT) (Deci & Ryan, 2012). There are three factors for SDT - autonomy, relatedness and competence. If these three factors are achieved, then the likelihood that the athlete will want to do this and engage in SDT is high, which leads to greater results. Fortunately for us, VBT and SDT go hand-in-hand when the program is properly planned and the coach does a great job.

Competence is crucial. The athlete needs to be competent in the movement and confident in their abilities to perform the movement. They need to be able to go into autopilot for this movement. When the athlete does the movement, they like doing it because they're good at it. To utilize VBT, they also must have sufficient strength, and with strength being a skill, we can again see the relationship to competence.

Relatedness is also important. The movement has to be related to the sport. That's not to say that VBT can only be done with weighted sport implements. If athletes know and understand the possible transfer, and the benefit to their sport, they will be more likely to work harder on it. In my experience, if the athlete understands what they are doing and why they are doing it, they will go hard at it. If they are instructed to do an exercise "because I said so," then they are more likely to resist and find ways to avoid doing things. While most athletes do not like squatting - it's not a comfortable movement - by seeing the benefit that it can bring to enhancing speed, power and robustness, they do it without question and expect it to be done in most programs.

Autonomy is something that I struggled to provide to the athletes in the past, but when I did, the improvements in speed and power were very high. When the athletes have some control of their own destiny, then they raise engagement. With VBT they have control over the load that is lifted, and they have the ability to increase the load at the rate they are able, without a pre-programmed alteration. Beyond VBT, giving the athlete some autonomy over certain areas of the program, such as exercise selection (within limits) may be an effective use of SDT and increase the effort of the athlete.

I believe that SDT, along with the rate coding aspect that VBT provides from a physiological aspect, are what cause great sport-specific gains, as detailed by work from Randall et a,l as well as my own work in the area. An amazing aspect was that we didn't have to change anything in the program if we simply applied VBT and the principles of SDT. The intervention of feedback alone elicited better adaptations in the current program, which was cool, at least to me. All too often we consider the physical aspects of the athlete and not treat the athlete as a person. By making sure we engage the mind and whole person through the utilization of SDT, we can draw upon the greater means of enhancing transfer.

The Methods to the Madness

All velocities listed in this section are average velocity. To clarify, there are no listings of peak power in this section.

General rule of thumb

Every method that follows has a velocity. To effectively use velocity-based training (VBT), stay as close as possible to that velocity. The athlete isn't trying to slow the bar down to the speed. He is always using a maximum concentric speed of contraction to move the bar as fast as possible.

If the speed is too fast, add weight to slow the bar down. If the speed is too slow, remove weight to allow the bar speed to improve. This is the general rule. The athlete should always move the weight as fast as possible with good form. Let the velocity determine the weight.

Strengths by speeds

One key advantage of VBT is that it allows coaches to ensure that they are developing the trait they want to develop. Every individual strength has a speed.

So if an athlete isn't in the zone of that speed, he isn't developing the desired strength (Roman, 1986). For instance, to develop dynamic strength on the bench press, an athlete needs to move the bar at approximately 0.8–1.0 meters/second (m/s). If an athlete is moving the bar too slowly or too quickly, he isn't developing the desired trait (J. Bryan Mann, Ivey, & Sayers, 2015).

VELOCITY ZONES

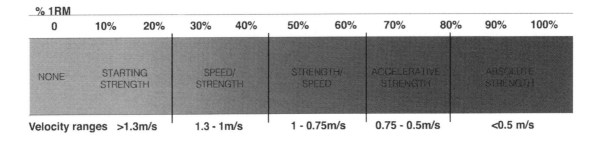

Figure 9. The basic velocity zones for the big rock exercises.

Until we have completely nailed down velocities to one-rep maxes for the various exercises, I will recommend zones. The zones have been set up for what were most often considered the big rock exercises of the time: the back squat, deadlift and bench press. While the zones are not perfect, they are quite close. I am working to look at relationships between velocity and one-rep maxes for a multitude of exercises. Hopefully, by the fourth edition, I have this figured out. It takes lots of time and lots of willing subjects to get this done. If your big rock exercises don't meet mine, that's OK. Start establishing velocity profiles up to a 1RM for your athletes, and in a few cycles, you'll have zones set up for yourself. Some people have identified squats, bench rows or biceps curls as their big rock exercises that they want to use velocity on. I apologize, but it just isn't going to work out for that.

The different strengths are as follows: absolute strength, accelerative strength, strength-speed, speed-strength and starting strength. By understanding what strength is being developed, the coach is better able to utilize the principle that governs all training, which is known as the Specific Adaptations to Imposed Demands (SAID) principle. This principle states that the only adaptations made will be the ones directly connected to that training. For instance, if all the training that is done is to improve the athletes' aerobic capacity in terms of a three-mile time, there will be no positive adaptation and possibly a maladaptation of alactic power.

Different sports require different traits, and different athletes will need different traits to improve in their respective sports. By utilizing velocity to pinpoint what those exact traits are and how they should be trained, the SAID principle can be further encouraged as a result of knowing and understanding this. Some people refer to functional hypertrophy as hypertrophy that serves the purpose of improving performance. By utilizing the appropriate velocities on the appropriate exercises, any additional muscle mass that is developed should be involved in a transfer to the sporting activity.

Absolute strength is developed from 0.5 m/s and below. Absolute strength is defined as the absolute maximum of what someone can do on any given day. Absolute strength is the strength that is developed when training for, or determined when, testing a 1RM. Absolute strength is most commonly referred to as strength. While it is a fundamental portion of strength training and the basis for all traits that follow it, it is not the sole capability to develop. This is a thought of the past, and research has found that continuing to increase absolute strength beyond a threshold or training age did not increase the transfer to sprinting, jumping and change of direction. During the first year of strength training, with massive increases in strength on the back squat, clean and bench press, there were improvements in speed, agility and explosive power as measured by the 40-yard dash, the pro-agility shuttle and the vertical jump. After this first year, while there was continued improvement on the strength movements, there was no improvement on the speed, agility or power tests. Again, if the athlete is moving the bar too slowly or too quickly, he isn't developing the desired trait.

Accelerative strength occurs when the barbell is moving approximately 0.5–0.75 m/s. Common vernacular has led people to believe that this is the strength that improves an athlete's sprinting ability. While this may be true at the lower levels of development, that is not the true depiction of this strength. This strength is best depicted as an acceleration through a load. Think of an offensive and defensive lineman in a football game firing off the line of scrimmage. The offensive lineman dominates the defensive lineman. This offensive lineman was accelerating through a load that was provided by the defensive lineman.

Strength-speed versus speed-strength

There was a very common misconception with this, and I am partly responsible for propagating it. In the original strength continuum, which will be discussed later, there was an unquantifiable zone. In this zone, there was an overlap of various capabilities, namely strength-speed and speed-strength. It wasn't an unquantifiable zone because no sporting results came from training those percentages of a one-rep max (RM) (40–60 percent). It was unquantifiable because the research team was unable to discern the split of the percentages between the two traits. Strength-speed and speed-strength were often seen as the same because they existed in the unquantifiable zone, and many (myself included) treated them as such.

However, when looking at velocity instead of percentages of a 1RM, there is a clear delineation between the two. Independently, several different researchers found that there are two different traits of strength-speed and speed-strength.

Their velocities are 0.75–1.0 m/s for strength-speed and 1.0–1.3m/s for speed-strength.

Strength-speed is strength in conditions of speed. It is moving a moderate weight as fast as possible. It has a higher rate of force development compared to accelerative strength. Speed-strength is speed in conditions of strength or moving a lighter weight as fast as possible. This trait has the second highest rate of force development of all the traits. It often requires special equipment in addition to free weights, in the form of accommodating resistance to achieve these velocities, as those alter the acceleration curve, allowing the lifter to stay in acceleration for a longer period and thus achieve higher velocities.

Starting strength is another strength that is often misunderstood, most likely due to the different meanings in the common vernacular. In fact, it may be better to change the term to starting speed, as this may be more representative of what we are attempting to enhance. Many people think that starting strength is developed by exercises like deadlifts or squatting from pins. These types of movements are developing absolute strength, but only in the concentric portion of the lift. This is not starting strength. Starting strength is the ability to rapidly overcome inertia from a dead stop. For this, think of a wide receiver beginning his route at the start of the play. The receiver rapidly overcomes inertia to be able to start running his route as fast as possible and leave the defensive secondary in his wake.

The velocity continuum

Many people have looked to different articles, texts and books for answers. In each of those different mediums, they usually have a bit of a different take on it, so what do you believe? In my opinion - and this is only my opinion - it isn't the differences that we should spend time on, but the commonality. As we just talked about with strength-speed, speed-strength, load velocity and velocity load, it's the commonality that we should focus on to know that we are on the right path.

Back in the mid-80s, a publication established what was called the "strength-speed continuum." In translation, the article showed us that some intensity zones for developing certain traits could be set up:

- 0–15 percent was neurological. You could do nothing to change that strength by changing in that zone. Provided it wasn't a drop and catch sort of thing, which is just working on muscle recruitment, it wasn't trainable.
- 15–40 percent was starting strength
- 40–60 percent was unquantifiable
- 60–80 percent was accelerative strength
- 80 percent and above was absolute strength

If we break things down, we will see that the same traits of the same name each have established velocities. Looking at recent research by Gonzalez-Badillo, we see that there is a great relationship between the velocity and percent of 1RM. Starting strength was 1.1 m/s, which equates to 40 percent of a 1RM. Sixty percent comes out to about 0.8 m/s, and 62 percent comes out to about 0.75 m/s, which

Figure 10. Utilizing velocity as feedback on a split jerk to improve speed-strength.

is the start of accelerative strength. Eighty percent is 0.48 m/s, which is very close to the 0.5 m/s cutoff for absolute strength.

If we look for commonality, we can see that when the athlete performs a lift with maximal intended velocity, it falls very nicely not only into the velocity categories but the intensity categories as well. This overlap gives one more signal that the categories of traits for both velocity and intensity are correct. Independently, the researchers found the exact same thing. This signals, at least to me, that we are on to something.

The Dynamic Method

Popularized by Louie Simmons of Westside Barbell fame, the dynamic method is used for building explosive strength. Both Mel Siff (Siff, 2000) and Vladimir Zatsiorsky (Zatsiorsky, 1995) found it an effective means for improving the special strengths. The foundations of Simmons' dynamic method are based on those methods found by Siff and Zatsiorsky.

The dynamic method can be used to enforce/reinforce technique on a lift as well as to improve explosive strength. According to Jay Schroedor, the great thing about the dynamic method is that while athletes are improving explosive strength and technique, they are also facilitating recovery. Schroedor touts training velocity as a recovery method because "velocity recovers everything."

While the dynamic method is thought to be for the bench and squat only, it can be used for any lift needed to improve sporting form or explosive capabilities, including the dumbbell bench or incline, the barbell incline, step-ups, lunges, deadlifts, horizontal extensions, bicep curls and many other movements. The only real consideration is that of the bar's velocity. To be part of the dynamic method, the bar must move extremely fast - 0.75 meters/second (m/s) or faster.

While there isn't any actual data reported in any journals or translated journals at this time, it is thought that there is a ceiling speed for an average individual of 1.0 m/s. If the bar, person or implement is moving faster than 1.0 m/s, it is thought to be too fast for a solid rate of force development, and more weight should be used to slow the bar down. Louie Simmons has found great gains by continuing on to 1.2 m/s for some power lifts such as the deadlift (Simmons, 2007). However, it should be noted that this speed comes after years of training by velocity. This raises an interesting question, which will be answered later.

For the upper body, it is recommended that lifters perform eight sets of three repetitions at 60 percent. Velocity-based training (VBT) can change this. We'll cover a few ways to make those changes now.

VBT changes for the dynamic method
The following methods will be explained as a part of the dynamic method:
- Ascending/descending, adjustment by set
- Same weight repetition, adjustment by velocity
- 8 X 3 set, adjusted
- 8 X, same weight, repetition adjusted
- Same weight and repetitions, multiple sets until there's a drop off
- Set total of repetitions, variable sets

Ascending/descending, adjustment by set

The 8 X 3 ascending/descending adjusting by set is a way to change the weight based on where the athlete is on that given day. This method requires intense supervision by the coach and a great amount of trust in the athlete.

The athlete will perform his first set at the selected weight. The second and each subsequent set will be adjusted off of the previous set's velocity. Of course, if the first set was too slow, the weight should be adjusted to make it lighter. Likewise, if the speed was too fast, the weight should be adjusted to make it heavier. For instance, let's say that you have an athlete who has a prescribed weight of 175 pounds for his first set and wants to move the bar at 0.8 m/s. The athlete performs three repetitions at 175 pounds at 0.92 m/s, 1.00 m/s and 1.07 m/s. We know that the weight is too light because it is being moved faster than 0.8 m/s.

So the weight is adjusted to 190 pounds for the second set. The athlete then performs three repetitions with the new weight of 190 pounds with the fastest concentric possible. He moves the bar at 0.85 m/s, 1.00 m/s and 0.96 m/s. From these speeds, you can tell that the athlete is closer to the optimal weight for the day, but still needs to increase the weight on the bar to achieve that optimal speed. So the weight is again increased for the following set to 200 pounds.

For the third set, the athlete again performs three repetitions with maximal concentric speed. He moves the bar at 0.8 m/s, 0.87 m/s and 0.82 m/s. This is in the optimal range, so you can choose to either keep the weight the same or slightly increase it for the subsequent sets.

The weights chosen are for those sets and those sets alone. There may be an adjustment made for the subsequent week, but those adjustments are insignificant in regard to the weight. The weight only counts for that day. If the speeds were slower and more within strength ranges, it may be easier to go on a week-to-week basis.

One thing that should be taken into account is that VBT is measuring power, not necessarily strength. So a week-to-week fluctuation of increasing or decreasing weight doesn't mean that the athlete is getting stronger or weaker. It's more an indicator of the current state of the neuromuscular system.

Figure 11. Utilizing velocity as feedback for strength-speed or dynamic effort work on a bench press.

The only way to tell if someone is getting stronger is by examining the trends over time. For example, an athlete going up 20 pounds over three weeks may just signify that the athlete is having a primed nervous system for a short time. However, a 20-pound consistent increase over three months indicates that the strength level has changed.

Coaches should not be tremendously discouraged when an athlete shows a significant decrease in the weight he is able to lift on a particular day. However, the coach should note this and alter the program because this demonstrates that there is a significant amount of accumulated fatigue and the athlete needs to deload.

Same weight repetition, adjustment by velocity

This method is fairly simple and straightforward. The coach predetermines the weight and the number of sets. What varies is the number of repetitions per set. The athlete simply performs repetitions until he is no longer able to produce the required speed. For example, if an athlete started out with a weight of 175 pounds, he would perform repetitions with that weight until he could no longer move the bar at 0.8 m/s. He would then take a break and perform the repetitions at the same weight once again.

The movement should be repeated over and over using the same weight for the duration of the workout. What should occur is a decrease in repetitions per set due to fatigue. If the athlete is able to maintain repetitions consistently throughout the workout, the weight is either too light or the athlete is resting too long between sets. It is recommended that the athlete rest one minute between sets.

Besides devices that measure velocity, a stopwatch is useful for this type of training because it's important that the proper energy system is being used. The energy system that is responsible for the extremely explosive movements that we want to train is the atp-pc system, or more simply, the phospho-creatine system. This extremely explosive energy system only lasts up to ten seconds. Knowing this, a coach may want to stand over the athlete and use the measurement device with the stopwatch to ensure that the weight is heavy enough for the set to be terminated within the ten-second window of opportunity.

Obviously, to track improvement you need to track the repetitions at the weight. However, like with the previous methods, don't worry so much about the changes from week to week. Pay attention to the trends over the course of several months. Remember, increases or decreases could simply be a factor of nervous system status, not actual changes in the physical attributes.

You might be wondering, how many repetitions are too many or not enough, and when should the athlete increase weight? Here are some guidelines to follow.

- Start out at 40 percent of the athlete's max.
- If the athlete is able to move the bar over 1.10 m/s at any point in time (if 0.8 m/s is the goal), the bar weight is too light and needs to be increased.
- If the athlete is able to move the bar at the desired velocity for longer than ten seconds, the bar weight is too light and needs to be increased.

8 x _ same weight, repetitions adjusted

This method is similar to the previously mentioned methods. The repetitions are performed in a set until the velocity drops below 90 percent of the best repetition. Perform eight sets and record the repetitions. The measurement device is not reset between sets to account for cumulative fatigue.

Same weight and repetitions, multiple sets until there's a drop off

This method utilizes the same weight and the same repetitions and multiple sets are performed. The sets terminate when the athlete is no longer able to get 90 percent of his best repetitions. While all of the previous methods (as well as most methods with VBT) use the top number as the most important number, for this method, the middle number, which is the percentage of best repetitions, is the most important number. For example, an athlete performs three repetitions with 175 pounds, and the speed of his best repetition is 1.0 m/s. He should continue to perform sets of three repetitions until he can no longer achieve 90 percent of 1.0 m/s or 0.90 m/s. Any repetition that drops below the 0.90 m/s terminates the workout.

Again, if the athlete is able to move the bar over 1.10 m/s, the weight is too light and needs to be increased. If the athlete is able to perform ten sets at the speed, the weight should be increased for the following week. Any large peaks and valleys should be noted and the workout should be altered, but aren't necessarily a sign of improving or decreasing strength.

On a day when there is a great decrease in the amount of sets performed, the workout should be altered. Instead of a heavy workout using assistance exercises, the assistance exercises should be performed with lighter weights and higher repetitions. This will help restore the athlete and allow him to return back to normal.

Set total of repetitions, variable sets

This method uses the same weight, and repetitions are performed in each set until the velocity drops below the speed. This method is very similar to the same weight repetition adjustment method. There is one difference though. This method has a total number of repetitions to be performed in the entire workout, not a total number of sets. While it's a slight difference, it's enough of a change to stimulate growth in the nervous system.

Band adjustments to velocities

When using bands for speed-strength work, Louie Simmons says that 75 percent of the total load should come from bands and 25 percent of the total load should come from actual bar weight. The velocities for the lifts will then change to 1.0–1.3 m/s on lifts such as the squat and bench press (Simmons, 2007).

In his book, *The Book of Methods*, Louie also states that for strength-speed work, the total load of the bands and weight should be equal,

Figure 12. Velocity utilized as live feedback for a squat. Notice the athlete's attentiveness to the screen, showing their competitive nature.

or 50 percent of the total load coming from bands and 50 percent of the total load coming from bar weight. The velocities of the lifts for this are 0.4–0.5 m/s. You need to understand what you're trying to develop (speed-strength or strength-speed) so that you know not just how much band tension and weight should be used, but also what velocities are needed. If you're trying to develop speed-strength in the squat with blue bands and 225 pounds on the bar, you won't be developing the proper trait because there is too much bar weight and not enough band tension.

In more recent years, studies have shown that using bands will increase both the eccentric and concentric velocities, improving rate of force development. This allows the practitioner to alter the stimulus to the central nervous system by decreasing the breaking time. Most likely, this will elicit better power adaptations than performing the same lifts at the same loads because of a decrease in the time spent in deceleration (increased accelerative time). Future research is needed to ensure what the training adaptations are, but the future is bright and promising for bands (Galpin et al., 2015; Wallace, Winchester, & McGuigan, 2006).

Bands are a fantastic tool for coaches or athletes to use and add to their arsenals. However, you need to understand how to properly determine how much band tension and bar weight you need, as well as how to set up the bands before you use them in a workout.

Dynamic method conclusion

An athlete's body adapts in about 3–4 weeks. Adaptation occurs more quickly in highly trained athletes and slower in lesser trained athletes. Because it is a coach's worst enemy, and results in sporting form tend to cease, it is understandable that coaches want to constantly change things in order to prevent adaptation from occurring.

There are a few ways to do this. One is by using bands and chains. By changing the accommodating resistance, you change the stimulus to the nervous system, thus providing another stimulus for the athlete's body to adapt to. This buys you more time.

For example, you could use the ascending/descending adjustment by set method. For the first four weeks, perform the exercise with straight weight. For the second four weeks, perform the exercise with chains, and for the third four weeks, perform it with bands. For the fourth four weeks, perform the exercise with bands and chains, and for the fifth four weeks, perform the exercise with suspended kettle bells. By simply changing the accommodating resistance, you'll go five months without repeating the same stimulus.

Progressive Overload VBT

Velocity-based training (VBT) can be used for a progressive overload strength type effect. This is extremely effective when using Olympic lifts and slower or strength type speeds on the power lifts. The same concepts used in the dynamic method apply here, but the difference is that these are done for absolute strength, not dynamic strength. The goal of this method is to move up progressively in weight per set from week to week while maintaining velocity. For example, an athlete tries to maintain a 0.5 meters/second (m/s) velocity on the bench press. He starts out at 165 pounds

Figure 13. Demonstrating the trap bar squat jump as an alternative to the traditional barbell squat jump.

and performs three repetitions at 0.65 m/s, 0.7 m/s and 0.68 m/s. The coach should be able to tell from these velocities that the athlete needs to increase the weight on the bar, so the weight is increased to 180 pounds for the next set. The athlete performs three repetitions at 0.6 m/s, 0.65 m/s and 0.62 m/s. This is closer to the desired speed but still not quite there. So the coach again adds weight to the bar. The weight is increased to 200 pounds, and the athlete performs the repetitions at 0.5 m/s, 0.55 m/s and 0.57 m/s. This is an acceptable weight and could be either performed for the rest of the sets or increased slightly.

This works basically as a daily adjustable progressive resistance overload. The athlete should try to beat his previous set on that given day, and by the end, also try and break his best from the previous week(s). The athlete has to achieve the desired speed on all of the repetitions. Depending on how the coach desires to do it, a few extra chances or opportunities can be allotted. So, for instance, the athlete might have five chances to get in the required three repetitions.

As always, pay attention to the trends in velocities, not the velocity on any given day. Be ready to alter the workout based on the weights used. If an athlete is having a down day, use lighter weight with higher volume or something more like a bodybuilding day. This may help the athlete recover for the next workout.

As previously stated, athletes only improve in explosive strength, power production, speed and other areas for a time, when the athlete first begins training. One of the keys to continually increasing explosive abilities is to continually increase the rate of force development over time. As soon as power production improvements stall, begin to implement the next trait up the chart for rate of force development improvement.

This section is very much theoretical for me at this point, and is based on what I have seen while training athletes rather than published research studies. What I have seen work the best is to simply move from the slower to the faster speeds and work your way through the continuum. While maximal strength must be constantly maintained or even improved to help reduce the risk of injury, the rate of force development must be increased in order to see improvements in sporting form.

The order in which I have seen improvements increase to their greatest potential is to go from improving absolute strength to accelerative strength to strength-speed and finally speed-strength over the course of a career. This progression has allowed athletes to continually improve power production and speed for several years. I have noticed that when you try to improve rate of force development within the athletes and immediately go for the fastest velocities, you do see an immediate and rapid increase, but you can't continually increase power and speed. It seems that one trait sets up the next in a pyramid style. If you jump to too high of a velocity too soon, you get a quick peak, but the pyramid can never reach its maximal height and the athlete never realizes his ultimate potential.

Olympic Lifts and VBT

During my first statistics class for my doctorate, I had to do a 25-page project based on the results from a regression analysis in my field. I thought I would do something easy that wouldn't require much thought. I was going to be really busy at the end of the semester, so I decided to do a paper on how the Olympic lifts had the greatest relationship to vertical jumps. I figured I'd fill in the statistical portion as I learned how to do it.

Well, it backfired. I wrote the entire paper, and then toward the end of the semester, I learned how to do the statistics. I ran them and was appalled by what I found. The improvements in the Olympic lifts not only had no significant effect, but the bench press was more highly correlated to the vertical jump than the Olympic lifts.

Figure 13. The high pull portion of a snatch developing speed-strength in this athlete.

This made me take a step back and examine things. We were doing Olympic lifts as an absolute strength type exercise with our athletes. Technique suffered, but as long as the weight went up, it was good. This led to nearly no hip extension, a great amount of back extension, great amounts of lateral foot movement, limbo style bar catches, and most importantly, ultra slow bar speed. Some athletes would clean and it would only be 1.0 meters/second (m/s) when we threw a measurement device on the bar.

So I thought, why do we do cleans? The answer was to improve explosive strength. However, the way that we were performing them, there wasn't any improvement in explosive strength. So we either had to change the way that we did them or drop them all together. We ended up changing the way that we did them. If you want to be fast, you've got to train fast. And if you want to train fast, you need a means to quantify how fast you're moving. Enter velocity-based training (VBT) and my familiarity with it from working at a few different places, talking to people about it, experimenting with it on myself and using it on athletes.

Figure 14. The clean is the most utilized Olympic lift within VBT.

I looked again at the translated Soviet texts, as well as the book *Weightlifting: Fitness for All Sports* (Ajan, 1988). I found the speeds for the Olympic lifts that we were doing. For a repetition to count, it had to be done at the speed required. If an athlete stood up with the weight, it no longer counted. The athletes had to stand up with the weight and do so with the proper speed. What happened was amazing. The sample size was small, but a regression analysis showed now that the use of VBT did lead to the clean having an impact on vertical jump. It went from fifth to third relationship behind body composition and the squat.

I want to just put this out there now - VBT in and of itself does not lead to improvements. You have to continually coach form, and make the athlete realize that the speed doesn't count if the lift isn't performed properly. The athletes are smart and very in touch with their bodies. They understand that by making a few physical adjustments and recruiting other muscle groups, or increasing the amplitude of the motion, they can get a greater speed. You can't allow this to happen because you will lose the results that you would've been able to gain.

Table 3. Mean velocities for different exercises.	
Velocities	
Snatch power shrug	1.45 m/s
Snatch power pull	1.81 m/s
Snatch from floor	1.52–1.67 m/s
Hang snatch	1.35–1.96 m/s
Power clean	1.2–1.32 m/s
Hang clean	1.3–1.4 m/s
Power shrug	1.15 m/s
Power pull	1.38 m/s
Starting strength	1.3 m/s+
Speed-strength	1.0-1.3 m/s**
Strength-speed	0.75-1.0 m/s
Accelerative strength	0.5-0.75 m/s
Absolute strength	>0.5 m/s

*Velocity is dependent upon amplitude of motion. Greater distances may result in greater velocities.

The velocities that follow are derivatives from Olympic lifting coaches testing Olympic lifters. This doesn't mean that they won't work well for other types of athletes. This is just where they came from. Some coaches have experimented and found that they get the best results when their athletes use slightly higher speeds. This is something that coaches need to experiment with to figure out what works best for their athletes. As previously stated, some have had great success with the following speeds while others have had to increase the speeds.

The initial use for VBT was purely for Olympic lifting to ensure that athletes were able to train to their utmost ability on any given day. It was used to help select the appropriate load for that time. As always, if the bar speed was too slow, weight was removed. If the bar speed was too high, weight was added.

For nearly every lift, there is a proper velocity. This allows a lifter to train properly by lift and strength.

Intensity and velocity with the Olympic lifts

Many people have asked, how does one change the intensity if velocity is the focus and the only thing considered? Changing the repetitions changes the intensity. For example, many coaches consider 85 percent of a one-rep max (RM) a 5RM. Likewise, many people consider 92 percent of a 1RM a 3RM. So just by looking at that, you can see how changing the repetitions changes the intensity.

Another way to look at it is you are always doing a RM with VBT. A coach wants the athlete to move the greatest amount of weight at the proper velocity/speed. By simply changing the number of repetitions performed, you change the weights that can be moved. Thus, the intensity is changed. Percentage-based training can be replaced by training with speeds/velocities. A coach can train an athlete for where he is that day, not where he was six weeks ago or where he should be six weeks from now.

Figure 16. The push jerk utilizing velocity as feedback.

The simplicity of just changing the repetitions to change the load is ingenious. It simplifies everything. It shortens the debate of whether a lifter should go with 90 percent, 92 percent or 93 percent for three repetitions. All that needs to be determined is whether a lifter goes for three repetitions. The rest takes care of itself. There shouldn't be any more debates about percentages. This in and of itself will speed up the process of writing the program. It helps some coaches tremendously, especially in-season, because they won't have to try and alter percentages. The athlete gets what he can get.

As previously stated, power is the first thing to go when dealing with overtraining (Fry, 1994). Because cleans are speed and power dominant exercises, they are movements affected by the stress of the season. By just training off the speed, you can monitor changes in power.

As with the dynamic method types, if the weight goes through short dramatic increases, it doesn't necessarily mean that the strength of the athlete has increased that much. It may just mean that the athlete was "on" that day. If there is a great decrease on a given day, the athlete should finish up the workout in a restorative fashion. It is the trend that is important, not a single day in the monitoring of strength.

By varying the repetitions, you vary the intensity and thus the weight. Also, if the athlete is unable to move up in weight from a five- to a four- or three-repetition day, it is a good thing that the coach trained with velocity, because the athlete wasn't prepared to lift a more maximal intensity.

One thing to take into account on some of the lifts, such as the snatch grip shrug, is that the velocity doesn't have to support the snatch. If the snatch grip shrug is a variation of the shrug, the velocity may be slower. If it is an assistance lift in order to improve the snatch, leave the velocity the same. If a coach wants to simply develop strength, the velocities can be lower to allow the athlete to handle some greater weights. The speeds for the clean are more applicable. However, if the snatch is one of the tested lifts and the assistance exercises are built to develop the snatch, the speeds should remain the same. The speeds on the snatch assistance lifts are such because of the speed needed to lift the weight above the athlete's head.

The use of the velocities makes it easy to perform a cycle of varying repetitions for the lift. A simple cycle of 4 X 5, 5 X 4, 6 x 3, 8 X 2, and 10 X 1 would supply enough variation to prevent adaptation while stimulating the explosive strength of the athlete.

VBT and weight for that day

Recent studies by Gonzalez-Badillo and colleagues (Gonzalez-Badillo, Marques, & Sanchez-Medina, 2011) have found some very interesting things. In their study, they utilized a pre-/post-test design for about 100 swimmers. They did a velocity profile on each of the athletes at the pre-test and again eight weeks later at the post-test. An average increase of 9.6 kg was found for the subjects, but no matter the change in strength, the correlated percentage of the 1RM to that velocity was a perfect relationship and didn't change. Stated in another way, it didn't matter how strong they got. If they moved the bar at 0.8 m/s for 60 percent, they still moved 60 percent at 0.8 m/s after the test. Between the pre- and post-test, the difference wasn't any greater than 0.01 m/s for any corresponding percentage of a 1RM.

Even more interesting was that this was the first study to show that velocities can be utilized instead of percentages. The study found that for this population, 98 percent of the people were ± 0.04 m/s for any given velocity and percentage of 1RM correlation. This also aids us in predicting what one's 1RM is on any given day. This is valuable because it requires no additional time. but can be tracked for progress over time and the fluctuations that occur from day to day. This was demonstrated in Jovanovic's paper, where he followed one individual over the course of an entire season. Utilizing a velocity profile, a 1RM was predicted for each day. It was interesting because there was such a large fluctuation on a daily basis, up to 18 kg on any given day. For instance, if on one day you prescribed 80 percent and it was a bad day, the athlete was attempting to lift 98 percent, which was far too heavy and could, in fact, push the athlete further down the overtraining corridor. If it was a good day, the prescribed 80 percent was really only about 62 percent, far too light to have the desired training effect. However, if the individual was utilizing velocity, that velocity aids in the lifter always using the appropriate load. From the Gonzalez-Badillo study we know that mean, propulsive velocity at 80 percent is about 0.55 m/s.

Systems like the GymAware track the data for you on the server. This is a fantastic feature, as you can see what has happened to the athletes longitudinally. Has your program been increasing their force output or power production? Has it had the opposite effect? If the data isn't tracked and measured, it can't be managed, and this is a real disservice to the athlete.

With velocity and it's trend for the individual person, you can predict the 1RM of a lifter within about 3.77 percent utilizing mean velocity, even doing so with submaximal loads. Below (figure 17) is an example of my personal velocity profile for one session. Knowing that my personal cutoff for the bench press is at about 0.15 m/s, I put that in the report on the GymAware. With the trend of the loads for the given day, the system utilizes that linear relationship to predict the 1RM. With the load increases and the linear decreases in velocity, the system predicted me to have a 430.2-pound 1RM.

Name: Bryan MANN

Gym : Bryan Mann

Date Range: 06/20/2015 - 01/02/2016

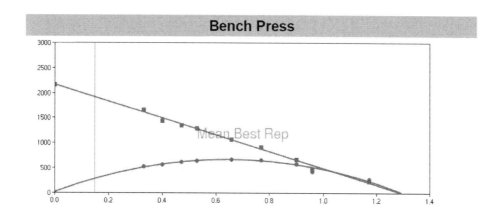

Predicted 1RM	07/04/2015	430.2 lb 0.15 m/s	
Weight	**Mean Velocity (m/s)**	**Mean Power (W)**	**Mean Force (N)**
45.0 lb	1.17	272.81	234.75
95.0 lb	0.96	428.16	464.36
135.0 lb	0.9	574.06	663.11
185.0 lb	0.77	656.85	916.33
225.0 lb	0.66	675.19	1072.55
275.0 lb	0.53	645.17	1292.01
295.0 lb	0.47	619.75	1354.1
315.0 lb	0.4	571.42	1437.23
365.0 lb	0.33	529.14	1657.81

Figure 17. Velocity profile and table for July 4, 2015.

Progressive Overload with VBT for Other Exercises

As stated in the dynamic method section, velocity-based training (VBT) can be used for other exercises. The main difference here is the speed. Speeds determine strengths, and strengths determine training effects. When coaches determine the proper speed they want their athletes to train at, it's very simple.

But first, what's an appropriate speed for a core exercise such as a bench press or squat, or really any exercise other than an Olympic lift? As a general rule of thumb, you don't want to drop below 0.3 meters/second (m/s). With many athletes that I've worked with, any repetition performed at below 0.3 m/s was followed by failure. The slower the speed, the greater the load and the closer to a one-rep max (RM) the athlete is. A true 1RM can be performed at any speed, but when training athletes other than powerlifters, speeds below 0.3 m/s may not be appropriate. For powerlifters, their sport involves standing up with or pressing a weight. It doesn't matter how quickly the force is demonstrated, only that it is demonstrated.

A general guideline for lifts is to move the bar at 0.3–0.45 m/s for close to max loads. This speed is slow enough to achieve maximal exertion and train absolute strength almost entirely. By training at the velocity and not simply standing up with the weight, you can look at where the athlete needs to be for that day, not where he should have been based on a number he did three weeks ago. This is a form of autoregulation as well as a form of progressive overload.

The previous week is used as a marker for the current week. However, that isn't to say the athlete must beat the weight. If the athlete isn't able to achieve the speeds for the weight he's lifting, he must decrease the weight. If he is able to achieve a much greater weight, allow him to achieve that weight. If he isn't able, he isn't able. The progressive overload portion is how the athlete gets stronger from week to week and over the entire cycle.

Prevention of Failure

Velocity-based training (VBT) can be used to prevent failure. Failure has been found to be very taxing on the central nervous system. In order to better manage training, train up to the limit but don't exceed the limit and achieve failure. Why is preventing failure beneficial?

As previously stated, it is very demanding on the central nervous system and thus difficult to recover from. A great portion of a program's results don't come from simply performing the workouts, but by ensuring that the athlete is sufficiently recovered in between the workouts. If the athlete isn't allowed to sufficiently recover, fatigue starts to accumulate. The accumulation of fatigue may eventually lead to overtraining. By not performing the last 1–2 reps, the nervous system doesn't achieve the same fatigue, which allows the athlete to recuperate more quickly.

An example of this is the 225-pound bench press repetition test. Hook the bar up to a position transducer. If the velocity drops below 0.3 m/s, stop the athlete from performing the movement because the athlete typically has 1–2 more repetitions left in him.

By nature of VBT, this is a built-in fail safe, and one of the reasons why many people achieve great results when they base their training on velocity. Because power is one of the quickest to experience a decrease in availability, we can use it to determine when to cease the training, either by the set or by the entire session. This may help to prevent the athlete from overtraining.

Determination of Actual Power

Matt Rhea, PhD, department head for the exercise science program at AT Still University, is working on something very interesting. Dr. Rhea is always on the cutting edge of performance. Many will remember the term "undulating periodization." In his studies, he proved that it was a more effective method for improving strength than linear periodization, but that's another book.

Currently, he is looking at the force of the individual athlete and how power is influenced by weight gain and weight loss. Time and time again, people have heard that there is functional and non-functional hypertrophy. Dr. Rhea is examining this by using a linear position transducer that measures average and peak power.

The use of the linear position transducer to calculate power is quite simple. When testing vertical, attach the loop to the athlete's belt. Enter the athlete's body weight as if it were a bar weight and have the athlete jump. The power output that is given shows how much force the athlete is actually putting out. This is useful over a multi-year career of an athlete.

An athlete may come in as a 235-pound linebacker and end up a 275-pound defensive end. His vertical jump may suffer from the weight gain, but is he able to produce more or less explosive power now? This is the way to quantify that. It eliminates the need for long equations using jump height, height, reach and other factors and will give the power. When tracked over multiple years, a coach knows whether the athlete is able to optimally perform at the heavier weight.

The velocity-based training (VBT) device adds virtually no resistance, so there aren't any detrimental effects to the jump itself. You'll get the best results using a higher capability device. You will get the peak power and velocity as opposed to just the average. Lower capability systems will track the average velocity and power, which is still good to know, but might not give you the complete picture.

Side notes

There is a time and place for everything. There is a time and a place for the use of VBT, and there is a time and a place where VBT doesn't have any use. When you're trying to build mental toughness within a group, training at optimal loads isn't desired. The athlete will never achieve an "optimal" load because he may not put out a full effort, which would determine a weight that is lower than what he needs to achieve the desired training effect, and thus never maximize his ability to achieve the highest results possible.

There is a time when coaches just want to push their athletes. Athletes need to learn how to push themselves and find out what pain feels like. There have been studies recently showing that an increase of lactic threshold improves aerobic endurance. Is it the training or the increased lactic threshold that improves the aerobic endurance, or is it learning how to deal with pain, understanding what it feels like, and learning how to push through it that improves the aerobic endurance?

When an athlete understands his limits and understands how it feels to reach those limits, he can learn how to push beyond those limits. VBT can measure a great number of things, but the one thing it can't measure is how mentally tough the athlete is.

Dr. Bryan Mann

Addendum

Since the publication of this original manual, much more has been learned and determined. More information is being published in various journals, and the author has been experimenting with different methods. The first is the relationship of Olympic lifts and peak and average velocity. Often as a coach, you believe that the athlete is moving the bar much faster than he really is when looking at average velocity. As mentioned before, flaws in form will cause a decrease in velocity. Sometimes flaws are just that. They are flaws because the athlete simply isn't doing the exercise correctly. Other times, there are orthopedic issues that stand in the way of correct form. Wrist injuries, elbow injuries, shoulder injuries and other injuries all play a role in the catch position of the clean or the starting position of the jerk. They also may play a role in the catch of the snatch.

It is also very difficult to measure average velocity for an Olympic lift. Peak velocity should be utilized for several different reasons: the ballistic nature of the Olympic lifts, the defined moment of a singular peak velocity, the elimination of extraneous information, and confounding variables such as orthopedic issues and the possible inability of the system to determine mean velocity.

Ballistic nature

Olympic lifts are ballistic in nature. This means that force is imparted for a brief time and then the implement is projected into the air. During the movement, the lifter accelerates the bar up to the second pull. At this point, the lifter stops actively producing force on to the bar and allows the bar to float up as high as possible. He will then drop underneath the bar. While the hands are, in fact, on the barbell at all times, when performed correctly, the athlete is only imparting force on the bar for a brief moment.

64

There is a point in the exercise when the lifter isn't actually increasing or applying force to the bar, so it is better to utilize peak velocity because this is what actually matters for that lifter. Taking an average of the entire movement is essentially meaningless because the lifter isn't trying to lock out or grind out a repetition when the movement is done properly.

With traditional movements such as squats and bench presses, the individual is always placing force into the bar, even though the neuromuscular system may be decelerating the bar in order to prevent injury. There is still additional muscular force being applied. With the body applying force on the bar consistently, regardless of acceleration or deceleration, mean velocity should be utilized in order to get an accurate depiction of what is going on.

Side notes

There is a cleaner number known as mean propulsive velocity. However, that feature isn't available on commercially produced and available units at this time. Mean propulsive velocity is simply the mean of the velocity during the propulsive, or accelerative, phase of the movement, and disregards the deceleration phase, regardless of the time spent in each zone. When reading and reviewing the literature, it should be important to note that mean propulsive velocity does give different values than mean velocity, especially when dealing with loads below 75 percent of a one-rep max (RM). When loads are over 80 percent, the time spent in acceleration gets closer and closer to 100 percent, decreasing the decelerative phase. Thus, the numbers start to achieve congruence.

In recent years, there has been a significant amount of research coming out on mean propulsive velocity, and the practitioner must be careful with his recommendations and whether they are for mean velocity or mean propulsive velocity. It isn't that these numbers aren't true or valid. They are just different than the ones you will receive from currently available units.

A ballistic movement is defined as an initial impulse force that carries the movement through to the completion. With an Olympic lift, the initial impulse force from the second pull propels the bar through the air. No more force is being imparted on to the bar until the body tries to reverse the fall of the barbell in the catch phase. Because the concentric phase is defined as when the barbell is being lifted and moved in the opposite direction from gravity, it is one measured phase, just like with the squat or bench press. Unlike with the squat or bench press, though, the athlete doesn't impart force during the entire concentric movement. Because of this, it is another piece of evidence to utilize peak velocity, as the rest of the movement during the pull and catch phase is essentially noise. The athlete is no longer the one doing the movement. It is the momentum that was produced through the second pull and that momentum is being slowed by gravity.

Defined moment of peak velocity

This is really an addendum to the previous point, but because there is research on the topic, we will let the research speak for itself. Harbili and colleagues (Harbili & Alptekin, 2014) found that peak velocity was achieved at the top of the second pull for both the clean and the snatch. This is the peak, and the barbell is decelerating from this point because the athlete is no longer exerting force but is trying to drop underneath the barbell or receive it in the racked position. This is usually quite a brief period in both time and percentage of the movement. Regardless of the lever lengths of the individual person or the individual mechanics, the nature of the lifts have one peak point, which is the top of the second pull. Because there is a defined moment at which maximal velocity is achieved when the exercise is done properly, there is one more vote in favor of peak velocity.

Elimination of extraneous information

Orthopedic issues often confound the results of the exercise. If an athlete has an injury or another restriction that does not permit him to perform the movement correctly, this will alter the mean velocity. Team sport athletes often have shoulder, wrist or elbow injuries from their sport that impede their ability to correctly perform the technique, specifically in the catch portion of the movement. These injuries tend to decrease the mean velocity of the movement by extending the time it takes to complete the movement, thus artificially decreasing the load to be utilized.

One other confounding variable for Olympic lifts and mean velocity is the way the mean velocity is calculated. The measurement system must know the exact moment when the bar is beginning and ending movement. With Olympic lifting, this can often be difficult to discern, as the athlete may catch the bar and return to the standing position. If the system does not recognize the finish until the individual has gone to the standing position (and this is included in the calculation of mean velocity), it causes the mean velocity to be lower.

Some athletes have distinct catch phases and then stand to the finish while others have more of a gradual transition or a soft catch that throws off the measurement system. These confounding factors cause additional noise that the system isn't able to filter out, causing it to give an artificially deflated number. However, peak velocity only reports the fastest moment and will not be affected by the catch. Without the confounding information to worry about, peak velocity ends up being a "cleaner" number from which to train. However, because the lifts that utilize a more simple technique don't have these measurement issues, they can utilize the more stable mean velocity metric.

When Olympic lifts are performed properly, there will be a strong relationship between peak and mean velocity. Most team sports utilize Olympic lifts as a form of general physical preparedness (GPP) to improve their sporting form. Olympic weightlifters utilize Olympic lifts as a form of specific physical preparedness for their sport. Just as golfers spend hours perfecting their swings and putts, Olympic weightlifters spend hours perfecting their pulls and catches. Expecting team sport athletes to perform cleans or snatches perfectly when they only do it once or twice a week is like expecting Olympic lifters to have a perfect golf drive when they only do it a few times a year.

Team sport athletes often seem to do a pretty good job with the pulls, but they tend to lose their technique during the catch phase of the movement. This may be due to purely technical issues, muscular adaptations for their sport or orthopedic issues. While some coaches harp on technique and work to perfect the lift, others coaches throw the baby out with the bath water and get rid of the tool. Before doing this, it is important to have regard for the purpose and benefit of Olympic lifts.

In my opinion — and it is just that, my opinion — we get the most bang for our buck with peak velocity measures in Olympic lifts. Peak velocity tends to better represent the capabilities of the athlete. The confounding variables are removed and what remains is all that is needed.

- Snatch, 1.6–2.5 m/s velocity
- Clean, 1.55–1.85 m/s velocity
- Jerk, 1.38–1.8 m/s velocity

Form

With Olympic lifts, you need to pay attention to form first, velocity second and load third. If form is off, you aren't performing the correct exercise. For example, if the athlete is utilizing lumbar rather than hip extension, it isn't truly being done for its purpose. It is important to ensure that proficient technique is utilized during the movement. What tends to happen is that athletes figure out how to get their highest velocities possible and they do it through an alteration in form. They'll try to pull with the arms or hips or do something else funky to accelerate the bar. Those with weaker legs might try to pull with their arms as well. Eliminate these fundamental mistakes to develop the appropriate trait in the appropriate manner.

After the form is sound, look at the velocity. Is the velocity appropriate for what you are trying to develop? Is it too high? Is it too low? Adjust the weight accordingly to ensure that the athlete remains in the proper zone for development.

Regardless of what the velocity reads, the form must be correct. Some have asked, "What do I do if the speed was fast enough to move up, but the form looked wrong?" Don't let the athlete move up. Fix the technique. The goal is transfer to the sporting activity, not just bar velocity. If the athlete is achieving velocities with something that won't transfer, the movement is pointless.

I have often said that the velocity measuring device serves as another coach on the floor. However, it serves as *another* coach on the floor, not *the* coach on the floor. You still must do your job to ensure quality and safety. The athlete knows that he must achieve two parameters in order for the lift to count: perform the lift and achieve the appropriate velocity. If he doesn't perform the lift because the technique isn't proper, he didn't achieve both parameters, so the lift isn't considered successful.

Height

Peak velocities, as well as mean velocities, will vary by height. The taller the person, the longer his lever arms and the longer he can stay in a force development phase. Before realizing this, we had one set velocity for all our players. For example, if we had two players, one a five-foot, five-inch running back and one a six-foot, seven-inch tackle, they both performed cleans at the same velocity. The running back improved his power output, and we saw what we were expecting in terms of training status. However, the tackle decreased in power output and started overtraining very rapidly. What happened? The tackle was performing the movement too heavily and too slowly, thus he wasn't seeing the improvements in power that we expected. The stimulus of going supramaximal on the clean also wreaked havoc on his nervous system, which sent him into overtraining. In order to keep the loads and velocities appropriate, it is best to have the shorter athletes utilize the slower velocities and the taller athletes utilize the faster ones.

If one has a great understanding of powerlifting, not surprisingly, height doesn't have as great of an impact on velocity of exercises like the squat and bench press as we might expect (Helms et al., 2017)). It isn't until one is on extremes of either side, very short or very tall, that there seems to be some issues. One reason for this may be that everyone is able to go with a self-selected hand or foot placement, depending upon the exercise. Taller people will naturally take a wider stance, and this wider stance will essentially reduce the length of the femur vertically (ie - in terms of a vertical force vector, you aren't actually sawing off part of the femur to make it shorter). A caveat to this comes when people are taller than about 6'6". People can take a wider and wider stance up to a point, but at some point the width of the rack serves as a limiting factor. At this point, from limited experience, the numbers tend to creep up about 0.10m/s.

The stance width tends to only make an impact on the Olympic lifts, and that appears mostly with Olympic lifters with nearly impeccable technique. In work by Roman and Ajan, they independently found optimal velocities by height by Olympic lift variation. In a study that is currently being written, when dealing with football players with only reasonable technique, height did not play into the velocity, and there were no differences in 1RM velocity across all of the traditional height zones.

Here are the peak velocities separated by height that I have been utilizing recently. These velocities are at about 1RM for the athletes I've worked with, and you shouldn't try to go below this unless you are focusing on overloading a pull. I think that over the next few years of testing the 1RM on different athletes, we will have equations that will allow us to predict a 1RM. When that information is known, it will be published. Hopefully, this will happen in the near future. Some people have wondered why there is such a greater disparity in snatch velocity when compared to clean velocity. The reason is the distance that the bar must travel. With the greater distance of travel, there is going to be a greater velocity, and this may allow for greater precision to be exercised with the velocity cutoffs.

Again, I want to reiterate that these charts work best for those who have excellent technique in the weightlifting movements. When I have gone to help collect load-velocity profiles for athletes on the hang clean movement, I found that those with poor technique just tend to shift their feet extremely wide to take away from sagital plane movement by adding to frontal plane movement, and the bar path, or distance the bar travels, is roughly the same. In fact, for an entire NCAA Division 1 football team with a group technique that might have been subpar, the mean of the peak velocites of 1RM were 1.54m/s regardless of height. In all candor, calling the movement a hang clean would have been generous, but it fit the criteria expected by that particular S&C coach. A different team with very good technique had 1RM velocities that varied by height and were near what would be expected, with a height of 1.5m achieving 1Rm at 1.6m/s, a height of 1.7m achieving 1Rm at 1.7m/s and a height of 1.9m achieving 1Rm at 1.84m/s.

Table 4. Peak velocities for Olympic lifts by height.		
Peak velocities		
Exercise	**Height in meters**	**Velocity**
Snatch	1.5	1.6 m/s
	1.6	1.85 m/s
	1.7	2.1 m/s
	1.8	2.3 m/s
	1.9	2.5 m/s
Clean	1.5	1.55 m/s
	1.7	1.7 m/s
	1.9	1.85 m/s
Jerk	1.5	1.38 m/s
	1.7	1.59 m/s
	1.9	1.8 m/s

Some programs are Olympic based and have done an outstanding job of coaching the lifts, and the athletes are showing outstanding technical proficiency. These coaches will most likely not need to rely on VBT. If the lift is done absolutely perfect, the velocity should be achieved to lift the barbell to the shoulders. Often though, this isn't how it works. All that someone needs to do is view highlight videos on YouTube to see that the technique is actually horrendous. This is where I think understanding peak velocity and including it as a parameter can help. The athlete will be focusing on the speed of the movement instead of simply completing it.

The use of Olympic lifting derivatives can be a nice and quite beneficial alternative to the full lift (Suchomel, Comfort, & Stone, 2015). Because most of the benefits come from the pulling portion of the lift, and the technical nature associated with the lift comes at the catch, athletes can garner quite a benefit from utilizing the pulling derivatives instead of the full lifts.

Mean and peak velocity with Olympic lifts

Mean velocity and peak velocity both have their place. With Olympic lifting, mean velocity is a good redundancy to keep technique in check. If technique is perfect, the relationship between mean and peak velocity is so close that they will be nearly interchangeable. In college athletics, there often isn't enough time spent to perfect technique and still increase load, so the disparity between the two measures increases. What truly matters is the velocity of the barbell at the top of the second pull, so I would just focus on that and utilize peak velocity. It just gives cleaner data.

Many athletes will have orthopedic issues that will slow down the movement of the bar near the point of the catch, resulting in a much lower average velocity. Thus, the use of the peak velocity may be much more accurate than average velocity for Olympic lifts in these populations. All other simpler exercises should continue to use the average velocity, as the relationship between peak and average is too close to worry about trying to change it up. The same goes for the trait categorization.

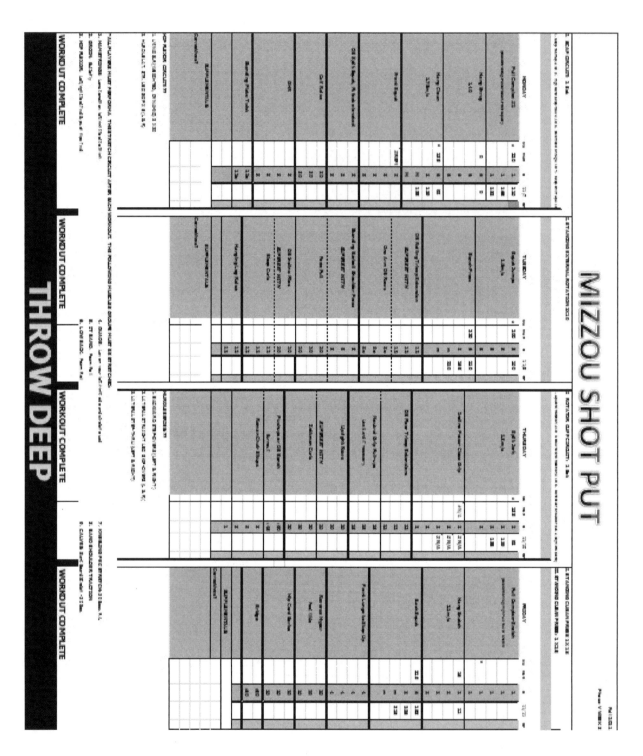

Figure 18. An actual off-season workout for a shot-put athlete.

The previous chart, figure 18, shows one week of one of my actual programs. My point is this — sometimes the pendulum swings too far to one side, and I'm hoping to show this here. All too often, I talk to coaches who have made everything velocity based. If you look at this program, which is in the middle of the off-season for throws, you will see that across four days, you only see velocities listed on five exercises. My main goal in training depicted in this workout is strength, not speed. Think for a second - whose book are you reading right now? Bryan Mann's book on velocity-based training, and he only has about one exercise per day listed with velocity. When I shift to a power phase, that may go up to six or seven exercises per week. That would be six or seven per week out of 32. So right around 20 percent is what the person who preaches velocity utilizes to train his athletes.

Is it a bad idea to get the numbers and measure things to store, to maybe use late,r or look at trends over the past several weeks? Absolutely not. If you have a system like GymAware that stores the data for you, by all means go ahead and do it. You may find valuable information that exists in there to explain various adaptations. The point is simply that it is nice to have, not a need to have.

GPP vs SPP and velocities

The velocities listed in the zones were based on a broad spectrum of college athletes from a multitude of sports from universities where I have worked. There was only one thing in common when examining the different sports - weight training was GPP for each of these sports. None of the NCAA-sanctioned collegiate sports are powerlifting or weightlifting. There are no barbells involved in the competition in any sport, unless someone is trying to elicit a potentiation effect, and quite honestly this may not be the most effective time to get adaptations from this.

To fully understand what this means, we must first discuss exactly what GPP and SPP are. GPP stands for General Physical Preparedness. To be GPP the exercises used must simply utilize limb involvement that is utilized in sport. For instance, a full barbell back squat would be GPP for a sprinter or a basketball player. The athletes utilize their legs in their given sport, but there are very few points in time where the sporting action truly resembles a full barbell back squat. To reach Specific Physical Preparedness, or SPP, the exercises must use the limbs involved in a manner that is more specific to the activity that is involved in the sport. For example, the lunge may be considered SPP for the sprinter as they are utilizing single and double leg support, and this may have a greater transfer of training in athletes with a greater training age.

What is considered GPP and what is considered SPP varies by event. Whereas the squat, bench press and deadlift are GPP for basketball players, lunging to various directions, drop vertical jumping, and med ball throws and passes are SPP. For powerlifters, it is completely the opposite. Lunging to various directions, drop vertical jumping and med ball throws and passes are GPP while squat, bench press and deadlift are SPP.

When someone is performing SPP, he or she is going to be more programmed and adapted to those movements. While most athletes that I worked with achieved a 1RM squat velocity at around .26m/s, Helms et al found that 1RM squat velocity in powerlifters was approximately .17m/s ((Helms et al., 2017). In a deadlift video, Chris Duffin achieved a 1RM at 0.08m/s, which may indicate that the longer the person has been training for powerlifting, or simply maximal training outside of an individual sport, the he or she adapts to being able to move slower and still complete the lift. When someone does this, they have gained neuromuscular efficiency which allows them to continue to defy gravity in those movements, while not moving as fast which will require less energy. It is beneficial for the person to be able to continue to overcome gravity and inertia without failing, because that is what will provide the largest 1RM.

The body always becomes its function. In some sports the athlete may tend to perform certain movements slower, or possibly even faster, than other sports. While the zones are a starting point, you'll want to adjust them accordingly if the athletes are in a sport such as powerlifting or Olympic weightlifting, where the movements are SPP rather than GPP. If neuromuscular efficiency of a barbell or dumb bell movement are important in a particularly sport, there is less room for error, and fewer generalities can be utilized in the performance of those exercises.

Velocity loss

Some recent work has come out of the University of Seville. Instead of looking at predictions of a 1RM or relationships to percentages of a 1RM, these studies have looked at velocity loss. We know from the work of Sanchez-Medina that velocity loss can be a predictor for a multitutde of factors such as counter movement jump height drop, and metabolic factors such as lactate and ammonia accumulation (Sanchez-Medina & Gonzalez-Badillo, 2011).

Another study that came out more recently from Pareja-Blanco and colleagues (Pareja-Blanco et al., 2016) approached the problem from a training perspective. This study went one step further and looked at repetitions performed to a certain percentage of velocity loss, and what the outcomes of training would be at each of the various velocity losses.

The simple findings of the studies were expected and unexpected. It is well known that when training for speed or power, it is the quantity of the load that is important. Speed and power should not be trained in a fatigued state, because athletes won't have the same recruitment patterns as when they are fresh, and could actually slow down or pick up bad habits. With that in mind, the results of the 10 and 20 percent velocity loss having significantly higher power gains than 30 and 40 percent were expected. However, the key finding that challenges our current path of thinking is the strength gains. As most are taught, training to failure is supposed to elicit maximal strength and hypertrophy gains. However, what was found in this study was actually quite the opposite. Strength gains were significantly higher in the lower velocity loss groups. It appears that the accumulation of the greater volume with the higher percentage drop off set didn't have the results that many practitioners would expect. This again goes to show the effect of quality repetitions.

In the following figure, we see the differences in cross sectional area and percentage fiber types and fiber areas. For hypertrophy, the higher drop off did elicit greater increases in muscle mass changes. This was expected, because it is the damage from higher time under tension that will elicit the greater responses in muscle mass. However, the study did note that with the 40 percent velocity loss, there was a decrease in the TypeII heavy chain myosin and an increase in the IIc fibers, indicating that the type I fibers were increasing. If the goal is selective hypertrophy of the type II fibers, the practitioner may be better off going with the 20 percent drop off.

	VL 40			VL 20			P-value time effect	P-value group x time interaction
	Pre	Post	P-value	Pre	Post	P-value		
CSA muscle fibers (ATPase)								
CSA (µm²)	4935 ± 690	5438 ± 788	0.02	4800 ± 691	5217 ± 701	0.05	0.005	0.77
CSA-I (µm²)	4314 ± 676	4798 ± 804	0.01	4070 ± 834	4346 ± 873	0.13	0.007	0.41
CSA-IIA (µm²)	5584 ± 1259	6233 ± 998	0.05	5708 ± 893	6169 ± 716	0.16	0.03	0.68
CSA-IIAX (µm²)	4619 ± 1022	5260 ± 962	0.04	4936 ± 740	5146 ± 744	0.49	0.06	0.31
CSA-IIX (µm²)	4406 ± 1037	4927 ± 1502	0.30	4130 ± 930	4853 ± 1016	0.16	0.09	0.77
Percentage fiber type (ATPase)								
Type I (%)	44.3 ± 10.4	47.5 ± 9.8	0.25	45.9 ± 15.7	43.7 ± 13.4	0.39	0.78	0.15
Type IIC (%)	0.1 ± 0.2	0.3 ± 0.6	0.87	0.5 ± 1.1	1.6 ± 4.9	0.22	0.34	0.48
Type IIA (%)	36.5 ± 9.7	36.4 ± 7.6	0.98	33.6 ± 10.2	38.5 ± 11.0	0.13	0.31	0.29
Type IIAX (%)	11.2 ± 6.1	12.0 ± 6.3	0.71	13.7 ± 11.2	10.1 ± 7.6	0.07	0.32	0.13
Type IIX (%)	7.8 ± 7.0	3.8 ± 5.0	0.04	6.3 ± 8.9	6.1 ± 8.2	0.91	0.10	0.14
Percentage fiber area (ATPase)								
Type I (%)	38.8 ± 10.0	42.5 ± 10.7	0.14	38.9 ± 16.3	37.9 ± 16.2	0.68	0.43	0.18
Type IIC (%)	0.1 ± 0.2	0.3 ± 0.6	0.23	0.6 ± 1.2	1.8 ± 5.3	0.39	0.34	0.47
Type IIA (%)	42.4 ± 11.7	41.8 ± 9.1	0.59	39.4 ± 12.7	43.8 ± 12.8	0.69	0.48	0.36
Type IIAX (%)	11.2 ± 6.8	11.9 ± 6.8	0.77	15.1 ± 11.9	10.5 ± 6.8	0.06	0.24	0.12
Type IIX (%)	7.5 ± 6.9	3.6 ± 4.8	0.05	6.0 ± 8.2	6.1 ± 8.2	0.96	0.15	0.13
MHC Percentage								
MHC-I (%)	42.8 ± 7.9	45.5 ± 7.6	0.30	40.0 ± 8.6	39.3 ± 9.3	0.77	0.56	0.33
MHC-IIA (%)	42.6 ± 3.8	47.3 ± 5.9	0.05	42.9 ± 5.4	45.8 ± 8.6	0.18	0.02	0.56
MHC-IIX (%)	14.6 ± 8.9	7.2 ± 7.6	<0.001	17.0 ± 7.4	14.8 ± 8.2	0.18	0.001	0.04

Data are mean ± SD; P-values calculated using Bonferroni adjustment. VL20: group that training with a mean velocity loss of 20% in each set (n - 120; VL20: group that trained with a mean velocity loss of 40% in each set (n - 10).
CSA, cross-sectional area; MHC, myosin heavy chain.

Figure 19

With this recent information, it makes the reader wonder how to implement it. The practitioner can set a drop off for whatever he wants. For strength and power gains, utilize no more than a 20 percent velocity loss cut off measure. For hypertrophy gains, seek more of a 30–40 percent drop off.

As a quick aside, some may see the shift away from the IIX fibers and become concerned. They may look at this and think, "All of my explosive fibers are going away from either sort of training. This is not good." I know I would have thought that, as well. What we have to understand is that Type IIX only show up in great frequency in elite level speed and power athletes (Serrano et al., 2019; Trappe et al., 2015), and for the general population are seen in the obese and inactive. For the general population, as one begins to train, there is a shift towards IIA, so this this shift away from IIX makes sense.

However, there is no indication of what is going on inside the body during the training. That's where a paper by Weakley et al (myself included) (Weakley et al., 2019) comes in. In our paper, we looked at velocity with lactate, perceived measures, and countermovement jump within the session. The participants did each protocol twice over the course of 8 weeks, and they rotated between the different protocols. An interesting finding from this (at least to me), comes from the reliability portion of the study. Most studies would perform the same session two weeks in a row, but in our study the protocol was done every fourth week. Even in this condition, the magnitudes of the standard deviations were the same as previous studies that performed the sessions in subsequent weeks. Basically, what this indicates is that the reliability of the individual is consistent over longer time periods. For those who have utilized velocity in training their athletes, this was already understood, but had never actually been demonstrated in peer-reviewed research for a multitude of reasons.

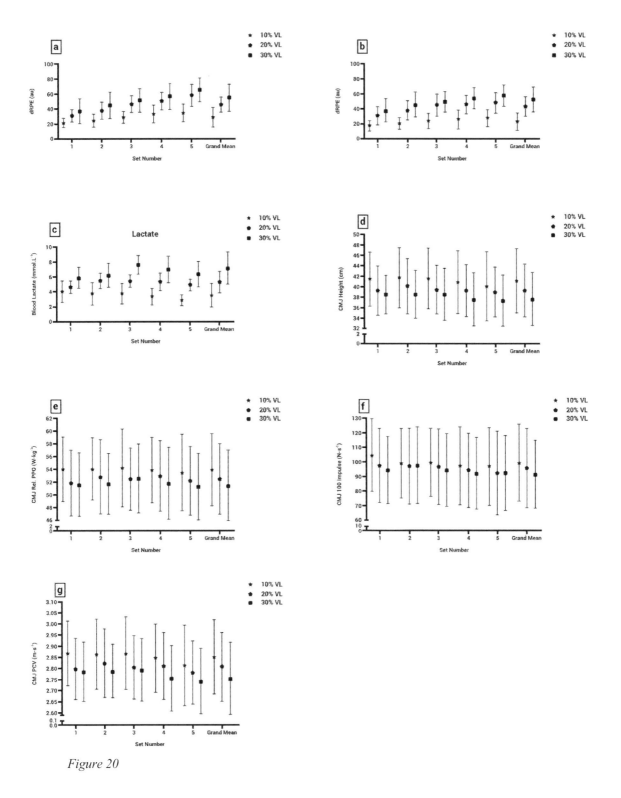

Figure 20

What we can see from this graph is that the lower the velocity loss, the lower the levels of lactate, and they actually tend to slightly decline through the first five sets, and actually increase on the sixth. This trend seems to hold true for all of the velocity loss conditions. This may be a result of the "last sprint phenomenon" where somehow, all of the athletes are able to run markedly faster on the last sprint of the session, even though they have been unable to stand up on their own due to fatigue for the last several repetitions. The RPE for the lower velocity losses was lower across all sets, of course. There was less work done, so they should not feel as fatigued. The relative power and peak concentric velocity were higher across all sets in the lower velocity losses, which is to be expected because there was not as much fatigue.

Statistically, magnitude based inference was utilized to examine how likely the protocols are to elicit a different response. The figure below shows that there are likely moderate to most likely large differences in RPE-L across the five sets between the three protocols, with small to moderate changes occurring between the 10 and 20, and likely large changes between the 10 and 30 percent loss groups for RPE-B. This isn't surprising because more work is going to lead to greater fatigue.

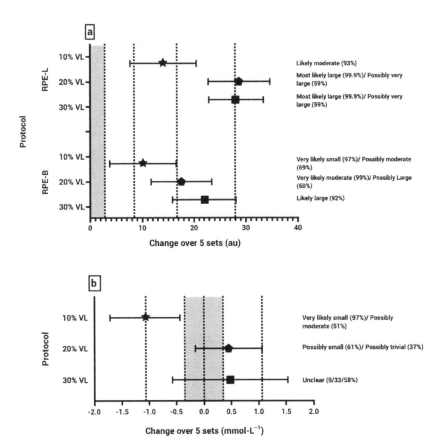

Figure 3. **Rate of change and corresponding inference across the five sets in (a) differentiatial rating of perceived fatigue in the lower peripheries (RPE-L) and breathlessness (RPE-B), and (b) blood lactate.**

Figure 21

When I first glanced at this figure, I thought to myself, "Wow, there wasn't a difference between the jump conditions." However, that's not what this is saying. Essentially, all the protocols found a level of fatigue and stayed there through the rest of the protocol. It is interesting that the level of fatigue stayed consistent across all the sets. This is most likely occurring because as fatigue accrues, you will achieve the velocity loss sooner and not accumulate increasing fatigue. Contrastingly, if you were to do a set prescription, as the fatigue accumulated, and the volume stayed consistent, greater and greater decreases of the jumping metrics would be seen. This could impact subsequent training sessions due to the accrued fatigue, not just the current training session.

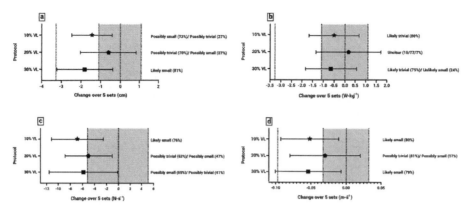

Figure 4. Rate of change and corresponding inference across the five sets in CMJ (a) height, (b) relative concentric peak power output, (c) concentric impulse at 100ms, and (d) peak concentri velocity. VL = Velocity loss threshold.

Figure 22

Now to get to the "why does this matter?" These two studies quantify the adaptations with different velocity losses. There is no "single best" protocol, it is all dependent upon what you're looking for. If someone needs indiscriminant hypertrophy, like an undersized offensive lineman, going with closer to a 40 percent velocity loss may aid them in becoming a better athlete. Even though it's not ideal, they need a greater mass to lead to a greater inertia to better perform their job. If the same lineman is moving in-season and you prefer to have set loads, you may want to go with a 10 percent velocity loss to control for fatigue. Conversely, if I have a sprinter, and additional muscle mass would slow him down and lower his strength to mass ratio, then the utilization of 10 percent velocity loss would be ideal year round. For greater tissue tolerance to fatigue, a higher velocity loss would also be in order.

There is no one way to train athletes. Each decision requires context. Hopefully this information provides you some insight into what the different adaptations are with the different velocity losses. When you understand what occurs with changes in power, lactate, and as a chronic effect hypertrophy, you can make the best decisions possible when training your athletes. I feel like I should end this section the way they would end the GI Joe cartoons when I was a kid: "And now you know, and knowing is half of the battle."

As a practitioner, when trying to develop power with my teams, I actually used two different protocols. During the off-season, I utilized a 10 percent drop off, and in-season, I used more of a five percent drop off. I didn't have these studies to back up my thought process at the time, but I felt that during the in-season I needed to stimulate power but save as much energy and adaptive reserves as possible for the sport skill improvement. I thought a five percent drop off would serve that purpose. I did this quite inadvertently, as I would say, "I want the first rep at about 0.85, and if you drop below 0.8, you're done." The fact that my gut instinct fell in line with their recommendation is reassuring. I think I made the right decision for my athletes.

With many velocity measuring devices, it is quite easy to use this feature because nearly all the different units have a "percentage of best repetition" feature. You can set what percentage loss you want. You'll see how it drops off for the athlete, and then you can utilize that number for feedback and to set your volume. While the absolute velocities may measure differently, making it more difficult to make 1RM prediction equations across a multitude of devices, percentages of best repetition should serve as universal.

APRE and VBT combined

The Autoregulatory Progressive Resistance Exercise protocol (APRE) is a popular and effective means of training today. It utilizes progressive overload dependent upon the person's performance, rather than a predetermined set and rep scheme. This allows the person to gain strength at their own pace, rather than forcing them to perform load and repetition progressions that don't meet their needs, but rather follow a thought mean of adaptation.

All of the different protocols can be summarized by the following two tables. For some, the APRE is old hat and they know it well, so I won't go into detail on it. For those who this is new for, please see the ebook "The APRE" on sale through .www.elitefts.com.

Table 1. The APRE routines.

Set	3RM routine	6RM routine	10RM routine
0	Warm up	Warm up	Warm up
1	6 reps at 50% 3RM	10 reps at 50% 6RM	12 reps at 50% 10RM
2	3 reps at 75% 3RM	6 reps at 75% 6RM	10 reps at 75% 10RM
3	Reps to failure at 3RM	Reps to failure at 6RM	Reps to failure at 10RM
4	Adjusted reps to failure	Adjusted reps to failure	Adjusted reps to failure

Table 2. The adjustment table for APRE.

3RM routine		6RM routine		10RM routine	
Repetitions	Set 4	Repetitions	Set 4	Repetitions	Set 4
1–2	Decrease 5–10	0–2	Decrease 5–10	4–6	Decrease 5–10
3–4	Same	3–4	Decrease 0–5	7–8	Decrease 0–5
5–6	Increase + 5–10	5–7	Same	9–11	Same
7+	Increase +10–15	8–12	Increase 5–10	12–16	Increase 5–10
		13+	Increase 10–15	17+	Increase 10–15

Velocity can be utilized as an additional parameter for a repetition to be completed with the APRE. This means that there is a minimum threshold velocity and the athlete must break that velocity for the repetition to be successful. This is especially useful when utilizing Olympic lifts or trying to build a specific trait with minimal time.

Olympic Lifts

Hopefully it is crystal clear by now why Olympic lifts and velocity may be a good idea. But if not, here is a short example of why they are important. If you have ever seen me give a presentation on VBT, you will have heard the story in full. Just in case you haven't heard it, here is an abbreviated version.

I had to do a project for a statistics class, and I did it on something that I cared about - the transfer effect of training. Before we learned how to do the statistics needed for the paper, I chose to write about how cleans related to vertical jumps. When we learned the statistics portion, I was on the road with women's basketball. So I chose this topic for the transfer, because Olympic lifts were a means to develop explosive strength, and the vertical jump is the purest expression of explosive strength in a single burst activity. When I ran the statistics, I found out that there wasn't any relationship between the vertical jump and Olympic lifts. I was floored.

There's a lot more to the story, but when you get down to it, we were loosely performing cleans. They were cleans in the sense that the barbell went up to the shoulder. The manner in which the lift was completed, though, wasn't really a clean at all. In fact, when we tested an athlete performing the clean, we first got a linear position transducer. We knew that the athlete should be moving the barbell at 1.35 meters/second (m/s). The athlete moved the barbell at 0.6 m/s. This was further evidence that we weren't really doing cleans at all.

We ended up making a requirement for a minimum velocity for our Olympic lifts. Then we saw the relationship with the vertical jump. Long story short, we got away from what the Olympic lifts were intended to do - develop explosive strength - and got hung up on the almighty change in the 1RM. By doing this, we lost the desired/intended training effect.

So with Olympic lifts, athletes must meet two parameters for the lift to be "complete." They must catch the bar in a rack position and stand up with it, and they must have a velocity at or above the minimum threshold velocity. If either of those two parameters are not met, the lift does not count.

Because the Olympic lifts are so highly technical, you should never, as a coach, prescribe a volume greater than the APRE3 beyond the two parameters instilled for the athlete. When you perform too many repetitions, the athlete's technique deteriorates and becomes something different altogether.

For example, let's say that we have an athlete who has an estimated 3RM of 200 pounds. He is performing the hang clean exercise using the APRE3. The minimum threshold velocity has been set at 1.5 m/s.

Warm up

    Set 1: 100 X 6; velocities of 1.85, 1.75, 1.77, 1.65, 1.68, 1.65

    Set 2: 150 X 3; velocities of 1.75, 1.75, 1.65

    Set 3: 200 X 7; velocities of 1.65, 1.55, 1.45, 1.45, 1.51, 1.38, 1.25

After set three, we would typically see that the athlete achieved seven repetitions and we would increase the weight by 15 pounds for set four. However, whenever we include both parameters, with the minimum threshold velocity of 1.5 m/s, we see that only three repetitions met both of the criteria.

Thus, we utilize the load change for three repetitions, which is no change.

Set 4: 200 X 7; velocities of 1.67, 1.57, 1.52, 1.52, 1.55, 1.45, 1.35

After set four, we would typically see that the athlete achieved seven repetitions and we would adjust the weight by 15 pounds the next week. However, when we again include both parameters, with the minimum threshold velocity of 1.5 m/s, we see that only five of the seven repetitions met both of the criteria. Thus, we utilize the load change for five repetitions and increase the next session's load by five pounds.

There is a significant adjustment time for the athlete. The athlete needs to change his focus from simply standing up with the weight to standing up with it at the appropriate velocity. The loads were greatly decreased when performing the movement in this manner. Most of the athletes' 1RM decreased by 20–30 percent. We had several athletes who cleaned 400 pounds but were only able to do so with the appropriate velocity with 280 pounds.

While some may think that the decreased loads led to a decreased training effect, quite the opposite was true. Whereas previously we saw no relationship to vertical jump, there was a relationship between the clean and the vertical jump after utilizing velocity as a parameter.

Accelerative Strength

Accelerative strength is the ability to accelerate through a load. While the term often elicits thoughts of track speed and acceleration, this isn't the case. Think more along the lines of offensive and defensive linemen firing out of the stance and battling for the line of scrimmage. They are trying to accelerate through the load of their opponent. I utilize a mean velocity of 0.5–0.75 m/s for many exercises on this. Much like the Olympic lifts, there is the preset minimum threshold velocity for the day and every repetition must be above this. I like to utilize a third working set for developing accelerative strength.

With accelerative strength, I most often use the APRE3 or the APRE6. I never utilize the APRE10 because the time spent for achieving this velocity utilizes an inappropriate energy system. The immediate energy system (i.e. phosphocreatine, alactic, or a multitude of other names referring to the same system) is finished within the first 10 seconds of effort. When performing 10–17 repetitions, you must go well beyond the 10-second time limit for the appropriate energy system. Then you are moving into glycolytic systems. Is this always a bad thing? It isn't if your intention is to build more of a lactic power capacity sort of thing. However, is that your goal? Personally, I lean more to the side of doing anything lactic during a conditioning workout rather than something in the weight room. Personal preference falls to the coach.

The following is an example of an athlete doing the APRE3 for accelerative strength with his workout based off a 250-pound "3RM" with the threshold set at 0.65 m/s. This is a three work set session with the work sets demonstrated as set three, four and five.

Warm up

Set 1: 125 X 6; velocities of 1.0, 0.9, 0.86, 0.82, 0.80, 0.75

Set 2: 190 x 3; velocities of 0.85, 0.82, 0.80

Set 3: 250 X 7; velocities of 0.75, 0.72, 0.69, 0.68, 0.65, 0.65, 0.62

We see that six out of the seven repetitions were above threshold, so looking at the chart for the six-rep adjustment, we see that it's 10 pounds.

Set 4: 260 X 7; velocities of 0.72, 0.70, 0.67, 0.66, 0.65, 0.62, 0.59

We see that five out of the seven repetitions were above threshold, so looking at the chart for the five-repetition adjustment, we see that it's five pounds.

Set 5: 265 X 7; velocities of 0.7, 0.67, 0.65, 0.62, 0.59, 0.56, 0.51

We see that only three of the seven repetitions were above the threshold this time, so looking at the chart for adjustment for the following week, we see that it's 0 pounds. Therefore, the next session will be based off 265 pounds.

Strength-Speed

With strength-speed, the velocity of the barbell should be 0.75–1.0 m/s. The loads become lighter when developing strength-speed. As a result of this, I often like to take additional sets for an increased volume. I like looking at 4–6 sets for strength-speed, utilizing the APRE3 or APRE6 to train the appropriate energy system. As with the previously discussed trait, there is a minimum threshold velocity chosen as a requirement.

The following example is based on an athlete who has an estimated strength-speed 3RM of 200 pounds. The minimum threshold velocity is set at 0.85 m/s. Sets 3–7 are considered work sets.

Set 1: 100 X 6; velocities of 1.15, 1.13, 1.08, 1.05, 1.04, 1.01

Set 2: 150 X 3; velocities of 1.08, 1.05, 1.04

Set 3: 200 X 7; velocities of 0.97, 0.95, 0.93, 0.89, 0.87, 0.85, 0.82

We see that in set three, six out of the seven repetitions were above the threshold velocity. Looking at the adjustment chart for six repetitions, we need to increase the load by 10 pounds for the subsequent set.

Set 4: 210 X 6; velocities of 0.93, 0.89, 0.87, 0.85, 0.82, 0.78

The athlete noticed his decline below the threshold on this set and decided not to do any more repetitions, as they wouldn't count. Four of the repetitions were above the threshold, so the load will be increased by five pounds for the subsequent set.

Set 5: 215 X 5; velocities of 0.89, 0.87, 0.85, 0.82, 0.78

The athlete again noticed a decline below the threshold on this set and decided not to do any more repetitions, as they wouldn't count. Three of the repetitions were above the threshold, so the load will remain the same for the subsequent set.

Set 6: 215 X 4; velocities of 0.88, 0.87, 0.85, 0.82

The athlete again noticed a decline below the threshold on this set and decided not to do any more repetitions, as they wouldn't count. Three of the repetitions were above the threshold, so the load will remain at 215 pounds for the subsequent set.

Set 7: 215 X 4; velocities of 0.88, 0.86, 0.85, 0.83.

On this set, the athlete again noticed a decline below the threshold and decided not to do any more repetitions, as they wouldn't count. Because three of the repetitions were above the threshold, the load will remain at 215 pounds for the subsequent training session.

Speed-Strength

The speed-strength zone is designated as 1.0–1.3 m/s. Again, the loads become lighter with the increased velocity, and athletes often do well with an increased number of sets. I often have athletes perform 6–8 working sets (for 8–10 total sets), again predominantly utilizing the APRE3. If utilizing the APRE6, cut the working sets in half.

The following is based on an athlete with an unestablished speed-strength 3RM and a 1RM of 300 pounds. Our eventual goal for each set is to be around three repetitions. Because this athlete has never done a speed-strength session before, we will conservatively pick 40 percent of his 1RM as the estimated 3RM number, going off a load of 120 pounds. The minimum threshold velocity for this athlete has been set at 1.1 m/s. The athlete will perform a total of nine sets.

Set 1: 60 X 6; velocities of 1.54, 1.52, 1.51, 1.50, 1.49, 1.49

Set 2: 90 X 3; velocities of 1.51, 1.49, 1.49

Set 3: 120 X 7; velocities of 1.35, 1.31, 1.33, 1.31, 1.28, 1.28, 1.26

Because the athlete was above the minimum threshold velocity for all seven repetitions, the load for the subsequent set will be increased by 15 pounds.

Set 4: 135 X 7; velocities of 1.31, 1.28, 1.26, 1.27, 1.23, 1.21, 1.19

Because the athlete was again above the minimum threshold velocity for all seven repetitions, the load for the subsequent set will be increased by 15 pounds.

Set 5: 150 X 7; velocities of 1.22, 1.17, 1.14, 1.14, 1.12, 1.08, 1.02

Because the athlete was above the minimum threshold velocity for five out of seven repetitions, the load for the subsequent set will be increased by five pounds.

Set 6: 155 X 6; velocities of 1.17, 1.15, 1.13, 1.12, 1.10, 1.07

Because the athlete was above the minimum threshold velocity for five repetitions again, the load for the subsequent set will be increased by five pounds.

Set 7: 160 X 4; velocities of 1.15, 1.13, 1.10, 1.07

The athlete noticed his decline and decided to stop the set. Because they were above threshold for three repetitions, the load will remain the same for the subsequent set.

Set 8: 160 X 3; velocities of 1.13, 1.11, 1.10

The athlete noticed his decline and that the last repetition was the minimum threshold velocity, so he decided to stop the set on the third repetition. Because they were above threshold for three repetitions, the load will remain the same for the subsequent set.

Set 9: 160 X 3; velocities of 1.12, 1.11, 1.10

The athlete noticed his decline and that the last repetition was the minimum threshold velocity, so he decided to stop the set on the third repetition. Because they were above threshold for three repetitions, the load will remain the same for the subsequent session.

Starting Strength

Starting strength is categorized by velocities of 1.3–1.5 m/s, depending on the amplitude of motion. Essentially, it is rapidly overcoming inertia, which is contrary to what many people believe based on the term "starting strength." They often think that it is improved by lifting heavy weights from a dead stop by doing exercises like Anderson squats, deadlifts, rack presses and other similar movements. For more information on starting strength, check out my article on elitefts.com. The loads are lighter with starting strength, so the athlete must undergo a higher number of sets to cause a stimulus.

Due to the high central nervous system and phosphocreatine demands of developing starting strength, I do not recommend the APRE. I prefer to utilize no more than three repetitions per set, with most of my sets consisting of 1–2 repetitions. The goal is to rapidly overcome inertia from a dead stop, not with the acquired inertia from the 1–2 previous repetitions. Utilizing too many repetitions would sort of defeat the purpose of training starting strength.

What do I do when set two of the session is way slower than it should be for such a light weight? There are two options: perform set three as it is prescribed and adjust for the subsequent sets, or adjust the load for set three down before attempting it. Velocity is a fairly linear relationship, and you will be surprised at how you'll be able to predict load changes off of velocity after a few months of utilizing velocity to dictate load.

Either method is completely fine because by the subsequent set, the load will be perfect. Utilizing method one, you may have fewer repetitions of the quality that you desire for that training session, but that's OK. For method two, you may over- or underestimate the load change and that's OK. As a practitioner, you will get better at it, and the subsequent set will be at the appropriate load yet again.

The APRE is wonderful for its simplicity because it adjusts loads for the athlete for any given day. One set will neither make nor break an athlete's career, and far less time should go into worrying about the load selection for one set as compared to what will transfer to the athlete's sport the best.

Choosing the appropriate velocity

For each trait, there is a distinct zone for most major exercises or big rock exercises, as I like to call them. Exercises such as the squat, bench press and deadlift all seem to be fairly close to one another in terms of velocity and terminal velocity, so you can utilize the same standard set of guidelines. However, some exercises, such as the front squat, overhead squat, and overhead press, tend to have lower velocities. The front squat will be lower, as you won't accelerate for as hard or as long (especially at lower intensities) or else the barbell will rise off the shoulders and strike the jaw/chin area, which is quite painful. As long as the velocity chosen is within the range of the zone, the appropriate trait will be developed. There isn't any one specific velocity that is penultimate within the zones. It is completely fine to wave the velocity from week to week.

For instance, if you are working on strength-speed, it is completely fine to change the velocity from 0.75 m/s in the first week to 0.85 m/s in the second week and 0.95 m/s in the third week. By going from a slower to a faster velocity, you are decreasing intensity and thus the load on the barbell. If we go from 0.95 m/s in the first week to 0.85 m/s in the second week to 0.75 m/s in the third week, we are increasing the intensity and thus load on the barbell over the course of the wave. It doesn't matter how the wave is chosen or in what order it is chosen. The only requirement is that the velocities are chosen within the desired zone.

When to cease the set

Of course, if the athlete's form breaks down, the set should be stopped immediately. Technical failure is always the overriding cause for stopping an athlete's set. Beyond technical failure, most coaches face a dilemma when deciding whether or not to stop an athlete. Does the coach stop the athlete on the first repetition below the threshold, or does the coach give the athlete another chance?

Over the years, I've found that the coach needs to give the athlete some autonomy with this. By the time an athlete is ready to work on special strengths, he is well in tune with his body and abilities. If the athlete simply falls out of his groove, I give him another repetition to get on it. This often happens with Olympic lifts. The athlete may fall well below the threshold for one repetition because he bent strangely or projected the bar improperly. The subsequent repetition may be far above the threshold, and the set can continue.

Conversely, the athlete may drop below the threshold due to fatigue or an inability to recruit motor units rapidly enough. In this case, the athlete is allowed to stop the set on his own instead of waiting to be told to do so by the coach. In my personal opinion, leave it up to the athlete. If the athlete wants another shot at getting a repetition over the threshold, let him. If he is unable to get it on the second try, I cease the set instead of allowing a greater accumulation of fatigue without the training adaptation desired.

The APRE3 is considered a strength/power routine. It can be done for either purpose, though this doesn't mean that a heavy 3RM on the squat is necessarily the best transfer to power. Some exercises need to be done very rapidly in order to produce high levels of rate of force development (RFD) and translate improvements from the weight room to the playing arena. Some exercises are best performed quickly using extremely light weight and low repetitions. This ensures the highest quality of work and most likely leads to the highest transfer to the playing arena. The APRE3 should not be thought of as simply a protocol used to get ready for a 1RM. It is also used with certain exercises to greatly improve RFD and, as a result of that, power.

Exercises such as the Olympic lifts, squat jumps, weighted jumps and the like are completely appropriate when utilizing APRE3 as a means to select the appropriate load. The main goal of these exercises should be the speed or velocity of the movement rather than the increase of the weight on the barbell.

One thing I have noticed with weaker athletes is that the load increases often don't work out very well. One of the major reasons for this is that any jump in weight may be a large portion of their 1RM or session RM. If the athlete's 1RM is 85 pounds and he achieves 13 repetitions on the APRE6, the chart says to jump up 15 pounds. While 15 pounds may not sound like a tremendous jump in weight, it is a 17 percent load increase. Furthermore, weaker athletes often respond well to volume, so I have slowed progressions for these athletes. Essentially, I alter the charts so that there isn't a 15-pound jump anymore. Instead of making the original five-pound increase, I have the athletes maintain the same load and I give them options of either 5 pounds or 10 pounds for the 10-pound jump.

10 RM Routine		6 RM Routine		3 RM Routine	
Repetitions	Set 4	Repetitions	Set 4	Repetitions	Set 4
Set 3	Adjustment	Set 3	Adjustment	Set 3	Adjustment
4-6	- 5 to 10 lbs	0-2	- 5 to 10 lbs	1-2	- 5 to 10 lbs
7-8	- 0-5 lbs	3-4	- 0-5 lbs	3-4	no change
9-11	no change	5-7	no change	5-6	
12-16	no change	8-12	No change	7+	+ 5-10 lbs
17+	+5-10	13+	+5-10		

In all candor, I often give the weaker athletes options. If they max out the repetitions of a given protocol, I give them the option to increase the weight by five pounds or 10 pounds but never the full 15. For anything less than the maximal repetitions, I have them either stay at the same weight or increase it by five pounds. It is their choice. If they achieve repetitions to the point that they could increase the weight for two sessions in a row, and they do not increase the weight, I make the decision for them with a five-pound increase for the subsequent session.

For the weaker athletes, their lack of exposure to resistance training often creates anxiety about lifting weights. I could battle with them and force them to increase the weight, but their anxiety may cause issues that result in changes to form or injury because they lose proper form. They may start despising the weight room, which may lead them to skip sets, repetitions or exercises. The best thing that we can do is create an environment where the athletes want to be in the weight room. We do not want them trying to get away from it.

If, as a coach, you need to change the program to a different RM, you can absolutely do that. The set protocols are simply the ones that have been researched and published. While this means that what happens to the athletes on these protocols is a known commodity, it doesn't mean that the protocols are unalterable to fit your needs. There is a systematic approach to any of the protocols. By following the base systemization, the protocols can be changed to fit any rep scheme that you prefer. Some people prefer 12 repetitions instead of 10 repetitions or five repetitions instead of six. This is completely fine. Just make sure that the adjustment charts are also modified to fit the new repetition scheme.

Beyond bar speed

One thing that my good friend Carl Valle talks about a lot is how body speed trumps bar speed. This means that the speed of the body moving is far more important than what the outcome variable of the barbell is. I agree with Carl in principle, but I think that it goes one step further.

Body speed is an outcome variable of training. An athlete can run faster and jump higher as a result of a properly planned training program. This falls into line with the principle called transfer of trainedness, which evaluates the change in the sport variable by the change in the trained variable. Essentially, did you get better at your sport as a result of your training? This is often determined by running speeds, jump heights and other factors.

Jacobson and colleagues performed an interesting study that we collaborated on and will eventually publish (B. H. Jacobson, Conchola, Smith, Akehi, & Glass, 2014). They used a linear position transducer with a hurdle to put a 90-degree break into the cord on an offensive or defensive lineman firing out of his stance into a tackling dummy. This change in approach allowed the researchers to examine what the body speed of the football player was firing out of his stance and how that changed over time. By evaluating this, it allowed them to see what the correlations to the changes in various exercises were, meaning improvements in what lift led to improvements in this activity. In my opinion, this is a quite novel way to evaluate this sports-specific action to see if a true transfer of trainedness occurred as a result of the athlete going through a certain program.

VBT as Testing

Force-Velocity profiling is nothing new. I assure you that in 1983 when the Kaneko study came out that I will reference later, it wasn't truly new either. But before we go any further, I think we need to take a minute and differentiate between some terms, as there seems to be some confusion. Load, Force, Velocity, Acceleration, and Power. I have seen some people talking about acceleration, and they are really talking about power (I know because their unit was in watts) or velocity (because the unit was m/s and not m/s^2). I have seen some people saying force, and they are really talking about load (I know because the unit was kg and not N).

Load is simply the weight that is being lifted. It can be expressed as an absolute load (how much weight is being moved) or a relative (sometimes called normalized) load (percent of 1RM). For instance, let's say that I have a 200kg squat max, and I'm supposed to lift 60 percent of that. My absolute load would be 120kg and my relative load would be 60 percent.

Acceleration is the change in distance per unit of time squared and velocity is distance per unit of time. If I were to run a 10 meter sprint, and my time was 1.65, my velocity would be calculated as 10/1.65, equaling a velocity of 6.06m/s. My acceleration would be calculated as $10/1.65^2=3.67m/s^2$. The point is that these are two different units, and even over the same distance with the same time will yield two different scores and thus are not interchangeable as some seem to believe.

Force is mass times acceleration (some try to calculate it as mass times velocity, and this is not correct), as Isaac Newton's second law tells us ($F=ma$ is the common representation). So whatever the mass that is being lifted, it is multiplied times the acceleration.

Power is Force times Velocity. While force mathematically is more dominated by mass, power can be more dominated by velocity. Because of this, I feel that it is important to know how peak power was derived - meaning looking at not only what power was, but what was the mass and what was the velocity. Let's say the power was 500W. Was it a 500N force and a 1m/s velocity? Was it a 1 N force and a 500m/s velocity? Was it a 25N force and a 20m/s velocity? While we are looking at some extremes on this example, the point is that force and velocity are players. Someone could be more toward one end or the other, and if we examine where it occurs, we may need to alter training to move it. If power is occurring too late (ie post 200 or 250ms), then we can see this and alter training to things that are lighter and faster to elicit power to be sooner.

I've said it before and I'll say it again, if you want a new idea, read an old book. Sometimes it's just an old study, but either way it gets the job done. I was sitting in on a class taught by Dr. Joseph Signorile. He has been around the block a time or two, and is noted for his work on power training with aging and diseased populations. He happened to show a paper from 1983 by Kaneko, and it hit me. If I just change up a small amount of what is done for a 1RM test, we can do Force-

Velocity profiles and gain so much information into what the athlete can do and what the athlete needs to do to improve.

If you are using a GymAware or another device that accurately gives Force, Velocity and Power at every load, this can easily be figured out. Also, from personal experience, you can set the GymAware up to plot these things for you, so this is why I specifically mentioned this device. I'm unsure of the others. It will require some alterations to the typical testing of the 1RM. With the 1RM, you are approaching true maximal force capabilities, so the force end of the spectrum is well controlled. However, most people start out at around 60 percent of 1RM after the warmups, and rightly so, as this is mentioned in most protocols as a good starting point. However, this won't give the maximal velocity component to see how the athlete is here. I recommend starting with a ballistic version of the exercise for 3-6 repetitions with either a PVC pipe or wooden dowel to get an unloaded condition to get a maximal velocity, and then a ballistic with 20 percent and possibly 40 percent of 1RM as well, to get a well plotted curve as we move into the mid range with the 60 percent of 1RM starting point. If I perform 1-3 sets that have minimal load and require minimal rest, I do tack on probably 2-3 minutes of training time, but I gain a whole greater insight into the way the athlete performs.

During all of these sets, from the unloaded ballistics all of the way to the 1RM, velocity, power and force need to be recorded from the device and then plotted. You can use Excel (but it does get tricky), or SigmaPlot (I prefer this one, but I only use it because we have it at Miami). I have heard you can even do it in R (Patrick Ward has done a Shiny App on his website, optimumsportsperformance.com - look for the article titled "R Tricks and Tips: Force Velocity Power Graphs in Shiny) and other software that is used for visualization like Tableau, but I cannot confirm this. When examining force and velocity, you will see that the relationship is curvilinear rather than linear (force rather than load is being utilized. Load-velocity is a straight(ish) line).

Once you see where the athlete excels, where they are deficient and where power occurs, you can attempt to develop the appropriate force or velocity end of the spectrum, or a mix of both. If you examine the different loads as presented from Kaneko in Figure 2 of their paper (Figure 23 in our book), you'll see how the interactions occurred.

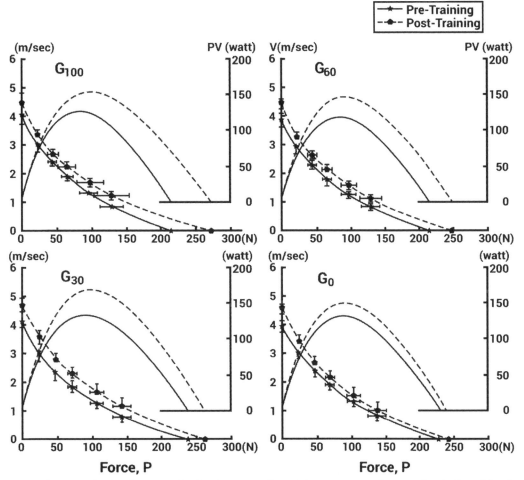

Figure 2. Changes in the force-velocity (concave) and force-power (convex) relationship due to training. The curves were calculated from Hill's equation.

Figure 23

The concave curvilinear lines are Force-Velocity plots, the convex lines are power-force plots and both are overlayed onto the same graph. If we look at the training at 100 percent of 1RM (for squats, dead lifts and bench presses, this would be absolute strength and circa 0.3m/s), we see that there was a massive improvement in force and a minimal improvement in velocity. Power did increase significantly, albeit moving to the right slightly. This portion of the chart shows the basis behind Bompa's statement that all strengths relate back to absolute strength - it is obvious that they do. However, the increase in force with no increase in velocity will, over time, cease to show an improvement in power that can be illustrated in the playing arena, as peak power increases do move to the right, indicating that they take longer to achieve.

This adaptation reinforces the findings in the classic graph from Hakkinen and Kraemer's GSSI 53, where they proposed that maximal strength continually increased force, but the ability to produce force in a short time did not improve. The 60 percent load caused moderate increases in both force and velocity, which led to a power increase going up and only slightly to the right. This sort of balanced training saw a similar increase in power, but did it as a result of increasing both force and velocity equally. This graph illustrates the focus of strength-speed and how both were enhanced through the moderate load, which would be around 0.80m/s.

The 30 percent load showed a significant increase in velocity and a minimal increase in force, but a great increase in power that went nearly straight up. Great increases in speed and minimal increases in strength show the apropos labeling of speed-strength, and these results are achieved at around a velocity of about 1.05m/s on squats and deadlifts (in the speed-strength zone). The 0 percent load of course showed great increases in velocity and very small increases in force. With the imbalance in results, we see that the power increase is small, but does rise directly above the previous number.

By examining the individual's load velocity profile, can we assign them what they need to improve? If they're good on force, we can start to improve their power by going to strength-speed and utilizing those velocities. If they've developed an increase in power by working here, they can move on to speed-strength and utilize those velocities. Only if they have gotten all that they can gain by using speed-strength is it a good idea to use starting strength. You can see here how the adaptations got their names based from what they develop and how.

Below are two tables (Figure 24 and 25) that are from data we have taken with high level Division 1 athletes using the GymAware. The unloaded condition was collected through the use of a PVC pipe and performed as a ballistic (ie they jumped into the air from the depth of the lift). The first chart is a spaghetti plot that is an illustration of power and where they achieve it in relation to their 1RM. This is normalized power to load and has everyone on the entire team to allow us to make more wide sweeping decisions. The fact that the plot is normalized means that the loads were based off of their 1RM and their power was based off of their maximal power as well. There is no load greater than 1.0 and no power greater than 1.0. With the information related back to absolute strength, force, and relative velocity, decisions can be made about how to train to enhance power in a more efficient manner. In most instances, weak individuals will improve their power capabilities by simply getting stronger. When someone is strong, they tend to need to utilize faster velocities to cause power to increase.

When examining the data below, we see that most of the athletes achieve peak power at around 60 percent of 1RM. Some athletes hit peak power at around 40 percent, and it appears that one athlete hit peak power at 100 percent of 1RM. The individual who hit peak power at 100 percent of 1RM actually had poor technique and was not allowed to progress with any greater load, which falsely made him appear to require maximal loads to achieve peak power. I did leave this athlete in for the illustration to demonstrate how this may occur.

Normalized Power to load

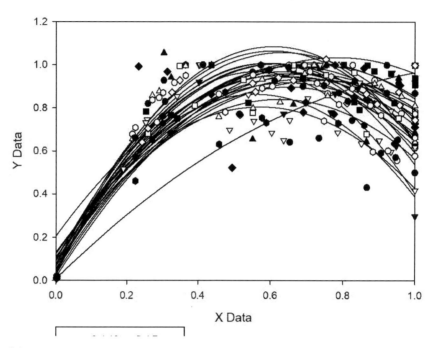

Figure 24

The other new "old" thing is utilizing load-velocity profiles for those movements that aren't the squat, bench and deadlift. I admittedly had rose- colored glasses on when creating the zones. I looked at this only from my frame of reference with the constraints that were dealt to me by sport coaches and my personal background athletically in powerlifting. They liked certain movements and only wanted those progressed and/or tested. Thus, I never examined stuff outside of the clean, snatch, squat, deadlift and bench press. Those to me where the big rock exercises. If it ain't broke, don't fix it. This, however, has led to some confusion when trying to apply other exercises, especially those that either have an instability factor or no ground based component (not even feet touching ground). Of course these are not going to fall into the same velocities as the squat, deadlift and bench press - the purpose of the exercise is different.

Load velocity profiling is basically what everyone does as a result of the Gonzalez-Badillo and Sanchez-Medina paper. Within a several week training block, the relative loads at the corresponding velocities are the same, regardless in the changes in the absolute loads. For instance, if someone is stronger for a session, they may be moving 15kg heavier for the same velocity of 0.80m/s, which happened to equate to 60 percent of their 1RM, so you can see how their 1RM is essentially up around 15kg that day, and the converse is true as well. If the coach happens to collect all the load-velocity profiles for their important lifts outside of squat and deadlift, they'll be able to derive their own zones for their exact team by looking for the mean and standard deviation for the velocity at each given percentage. Using their individual load-velocity profile is obviously the most accurate way of training athletes, but if you are beyond a 1:5 ratio, I have found it difficult to maintain this sort of precision and revert to group means. Also, you must continually monitor this. As a result of heavy strength training, you can achieve movement at slower and slower velocities as your body is adapted to be able to move these heavier loads. If you look back to that Gonzalez-Badillo study, you will notice that at not one single load were they moving faster - they were moving slower at every intensity. I've noticed with athletes that they seem to drop velocity by about 0.02 to 0.04m/s per year.

This may also be important for athletes of lower qualification but higher strength levels, meaning high school kids that are already performing full squats with greater than two times their body weight with good technique. The zones were collected on a multitiude of Division 1 athletes, and sometimes those speeds don't work for the high school athlete. They don't have the same nervous system, and things may need to be adjusted. Likewise for very specific populations like strength-sports - they have gained neuromuscular efficiency to move more slowly to allow them to lift a heavier weight. For instance, my training partner (who is known as Doc Dave if you have listened to some of the chatter about Westside vs. the World) would achieve 1RM bench press at about 0.08m/s, as opposed to the 0.15m/s that I would see in most Division 1 athletes, and Chris Duffin showed a video of him achieving a deadlift at 0.08m/s, as opposed to the 0.32m/s I typically saw in most Division 1 athletes.

Speaking of the individual load-velocity relationship, below is a load velocity graph for our athletes, again collected with GymAware. The velocity end of the spectrum was taken with ballistic movements performed on a modified PVC pipe trap bar. The starting position for this was performed at the same height as the high handles with the bumper plates used in the program. One hundred percent of 1RM was utilized as the force end of the spectrum. By examining the slopes of these curves, we can see if individuals are more deficient in velocity or force. These data plotted are for those who achieved a true 1RM, and did not include younger athletes who had difficulty when progressing to heavier loads and dealt with technical breakdowns. These athletes were stopped by the strength and conditioning coach because their technique was no longer acceptable and were thus at a greater risk of injury when continuing with heavier loading. I do not have normative data regarding what is optimal for load and velocity at this point in time, nor do I have an optimal slope or curve. We do see that there is a pretty significant disparity between those who achieved the highest unloaded velocities and those who achieved the lowest. There was a much smaller discrepancy in loads greater than 60 percent, and the line became nearly linear after having a slightly curvilinear design with the lighter intensities (less than 40 percent). It nearly appears as if there are two straight lines that intersect for the velocity end of the spectrum and the load end of the spectrum. With the plethora of data that is out there showing a curvilinear relationship, further collegiate data needs to be collected to examine if this is an issue of the specific population or due to the unconventional nature of examining the entire spectrum of the load-velocity relationship.

Velocity:load true 1RM

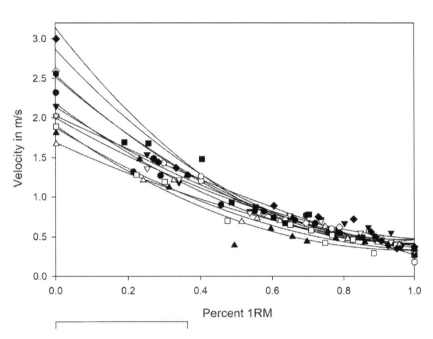

Figure 25

The charts I plotted were done in SigmaPlot due to the fact that I had access to this program and enjoyed its capabilities. After a short learning curve, the production of various curves was very easy. There are plenty of other programs that can produce data visualizations and will do an excellent job (maybe even better than SigmaPlot). Some people have made gorgeous visualizations even in Excel. Whatever you have access to is what you should use.

Now, one of the questions is what will happen if you start to train where the individual is exhibiting a weakness? This fear comes up for many when training something in a different manner than what they are accustomed, and is well warranted. We are comfortable when we know what will happen. I know that in my own training of athletes, I had an over-reliance on force adaptations when they weren't helping, because I knew how to train it and I knew what would happen. A paper that was spearheaded by JB Morin (Jimenez-Reyes, Samozino, & Morin, 2019) illustrates the adaptations that would occur and does it quite well. Here I am including a figure from that paper.

A

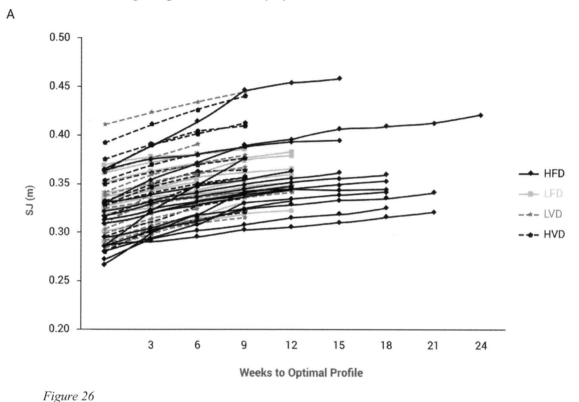

Figure 26

From Figure 26, we can see the adaptations. This type of graph is often called a spaghetti plot because it contains all of the data from all individuals and illustrates it in one plot that often times looks like a bowl of spaghetti. The Y axis is squat jump height, and the X axis is weeks to optimal profile. The training was individualized toward their deficit. Those who exhibited a force deficit did training toward that deficit - ie heavy resistance training. Those who had a velocity deficit focused on exercises that would more greatly increase their velocity adaptations with different ballistic exercises.

In most studies, you will see some people get better and some get worse. This is because not everyone responds the same way to the same protocol. Because these individuals were given a program that was to meet their individual needs, every subject improved. The number of weeks that it took to reach the optimal profile, as determined by JB Morin's force-velocity-power profiling, is what varied. It appears that those who had a force deficit (identified by the solid line and circles) required a longer time to achieve an optimal profile than those who had a velocity deficit. There were only four individuals who required more than nine weeks to achieve an optimal profile for velocity, with an equal number of high and low deficits.

Contrary to this were the force deficit individuals who had 18 subjects. It appears that the force deficits take longer to improve than the velocity deficits. This is most likely due to the type of adaptation that is required to occur for the adaptation. The velocity deficit typically requires adaptations of enhanced rate coding, which occurs rather rapidly because this is primarily a neural adaptation. The force adaptations typically require changes to the muscle structure such as a thickening of the heavy chain myosin. This requires a greater time to make the adaptation, which may explain why the difference in time to optimal profile was so drastically different between the two groups. It is interesting how everyone improved from this approach. This indicates that if you are attempting a greater increase in height, it is beneficial to spend a great amount of time focusing on your deficits.

This also indicates that strength should be prioritized earlier in the training period and career, becaused it takes much longer to improve force capabilities of the individual. For the annual plan, training strength earlier and looking at the conversion to power by the use of velocity-dominant exercises, supports the findings of many studies done on block periodization. where the strength phases are long and the velocity or power-focused phases are short by comparison. From the LTAD model, at least, when dealing with athletes who are physically mature, it is most beneficial to develop strength first. Great increases in speed and power are seen early and then level off.

A second wave of adaptation is then found when velocity is introduced as a primary trait. This also may speak to the effectiveness of concurrent periodization, where two separate traits (force and velocity) are trained in the same week, but on different days when focus is on that trait. For instance, one day would be devoted to improvements on the force end of the spectrum (like a max effort training session) and another day would be devoted to improvements on the velocity end of the spectrum (like a dynamic effort day). Once the force deficit abilities are maximized, further gains can be seen by using higher and higher velocity exercises.

What is good? What is needed to improve? These are things that you may need to find out for yourself. If you can categorize the athletes into different buckets, you may find that there are differences that exist for different positions or different types of players. For some sports, things will be pretty homogenous. For example, with baseball data, there was no difference between any of the positions, but there was a difference between those who were the highest performers and the rest of the team in terms of velocity.

For other sports, this homogeneity may not hold up. If there are large physical disparities and demands between positions, then there is a great likelihood that you may find significant differences. It may be necessary to bucket those positions before running the analysis. For instance, offensive lineman and defensive tackles have much of the same physical attributes and similar demands in terms of fighting for the line of scrimmage, so they may be good to bucket together. Linebackers, tight ends, fullbacks, and sometimes defensive ends are similar, and wide receivers and defensive backs and sometimes running backs are similar. When you categorize like this, you can get insights sooner. To find out if differences exist, you can simply run a one-way anova in Excel or another SPSS program and find out if differences exist.

Once you find out if the differences exist, you can examine what made an athlete succesful or not. If there are trends that the successful athletes all have, you may want to focus training to help athletes get there. For instance, with a baseball team, the differences lie in the extreme velocity end of the spectrum. If the athlete is very advanced in terms of force development but is poor in the velocity end of the spectrum, spending a greater amount of time on the velocity end of the spectrum would likely end in an improvement in playing ability.

In Figure 2, listed as (27), it appears that the changes stuck around over each of the detraining periods. There was a gentle sloping of the line back toward the original deficit over the three-week period that the subjects were experiencing follow-up testing. During this time period they would only perform the F-V-P profile once a week and refrained from any additional resistance or power training. While it is impossible to say that the changes are concrete and everlasting, it is apparent that they will remain for at least three weeks. The length of time that the results will be retained is currently unknown. However, we can say that if one is tapering for the results of a major competition, the resulting adaptation will most likely be retained during that taper.

B

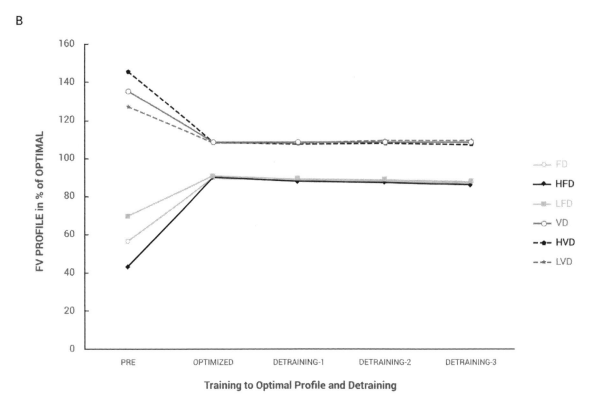

Figure 27

So when we determine what the deficiency is, we have a multitude of means to approach the rectification of these issues. The first is through the use of feedback and load-velocity profiles where strength-speed is the primary focus, and then speed-strength if the subsequent velocity adaptations have not been made. Loaded jump squats are also a fantastic means. They could either be performed as a full range of motion squat and done balistically or at a self-selected depth. These are two different variants that have two potentially different adaptations, as illustrated by Rhea et al in their examination on squat depth and how much transfer occurred over to sprints and jumps {Rhea, 2016 #1295}. This is most likely due to biomechanical and joint angle specificity. Most individuals don't jump from a full squat, they jump from somewhere more near a quarter or half squat. As we found, using trained athletes who already possessed the requisite strength levels, the training at the joint angles involved in the activity led to the greatest improvements of the activity. In other words, this study found that the quarter squat had the greatest carryover to jump and sprint improvement, followed by the half and then full squat. This is not to say that the full squat didn't improve jumping and sprinting ability. It absolutely did, it just didn't improve to the extent that the shallower activities did.

This leads us to the next important point, that we may need to further examine the use of special exercises. Seen in figure 28 is the change that our athletes went through over the course of their careers, and we examined these results over a period of 15 years. The Y axis is a percentage of power per unit of body weight as compared to when they entered the program. We looked at this in relative terms to account for changes that may happen in body weight. Power was calculated using the Sayers equation for vertical jump {Sayers SP, 1999 #244}. The traditional is the percentage-based program when everyone performed the same program. The levels incorporate the use of velocity-based training. We can see that the levels had a greater increase in power than the traditional, although it did eventually level off. We did not perform FVP with the athletes during this period because we were not aware of its existence. We did, however, use some sort of profiling looking at a ratio between strength and power, a bastardized version of Zatsiorsky's explosive strength deficit where we looked at the results of the Sayers equation and divided it by their 1RM squat plus body weight. This was the only evaluation that was done, if we felt they needed more strength or more speed to their training. While it was not super scientific, we did feel it helped us guide our program.

Now, examining Figure 28, we see that the levels did in fact plateau. We only utilized strength-speed for these athletes; the increase to speed-strength would have most likely furthered the increase in power that we saw, but we don't know for sure. I am also sure that this increase would have also leveled off, and the utilization of different exercises would have further stimulated adaptations in the velocity end of the spectrum. This would be in line with further jumping activities, plyometric activities, resisted jumping, etc. There would also possily be an additional increase by changing Olympic style weightlifting movements and their derivatives from the clean and its variants to the snatch and its variants, because the snatch utilizes higher velocities to perform the movements due to its increased range of motion. In addition to these changes, the addition of other special exercises to provide joint specific, joint angle specific and movement specific adaptations may have been well utilized. The utilization of different squatting variants as they increase in mastery may have had additional gains when training the force end of the spectrum and sequentially the velocity end of the spectrum. The utilization of different force vectors from cables or bands. to more mimic how the body acts during activities such as in a horizontally resisted forward or lateral lunge, also would have most likely given additional adaptations.

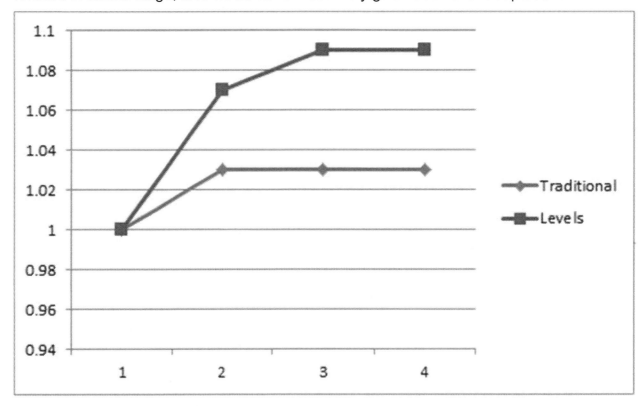

Figure 28

I strongly feel that the addition of the special exercises and additional velocity metrics and changes to the variants of the Olympic movements would have continued to increase the power ability for the entire year. To be direct and blunt, if the only activity that is performed is the main lift and done for different velocities, there are a lot of possible adaptations that are left on the table. Utilize a multitude of different exercises to maximize performance. If you continue to perform an exercise for strength and no longer see adaptations in it, try it for speed. If you train the exercise for speed and no longer see adaptations in power or running velocity from it, utilize a more specific variant. It is well known that general movements produce specific adaptations for the lesser trained athletes. As athletes increase in their training age, specificity must increase.

One other area within the FVP that may be extremely useful is in the determination of actual strength and force capabilities. When testing a Division 1 baseball team, we would cease the testing session for an individual when the form was no longer acceptable, per recommendations from the NSCA Essentials of Strength & Conditioning (Haff & Triplett, 2015)). When we examined their Force-Velocity profile, as you can see in Figure __, what was considered their 1RM was completed at a velocity greater than 0.5m/s. This is on average approximately 80 percent of 1RM. We are often told that 1RM moves up quickly because of neural adaptations, and this may well be true, but I now would argue that these athletes are not expressing their maximum force capability due to a lack of efficiency in the motor pattern of the movement, rather than in ability. So this begs the question, is it really that common for an individual's maximum to increase to that great of an extent during the first years of training because they improved their force capability, or because they improved their efficiency of the motor pattern? The athletes who achieved a true 1RM did so at approximately 13 percent of maximum velocity, whereas the group that did not achieve a true 1RM as we defined it did so at approximately 23 percent of maximum velocity.

So then, is the testing of 1RM for lesser trained athletes even the gold standard for strength measures? It would appear not. To gain further insight, we could potentially do one of two things. The first may be to use a predicted 1RM, similar to the approach from Jovanovic and Flanagan (Jovanovic, 2014), and utilize this rather than a tested 1RM for comparison against their subsequent testing sessions, to see what changes occurred to know if the program were successful or not. The subsequent tests should allow us to understand what changes in force capabilities occurred. This of course is relying on estimations of maximal force rather than the measurement of maximal force, so there may be some inaccuracy as a result of this. During this time, the athletes must continue to use submaximal loads, and hopefully ones that are heavier and leaning toward maximal loading, to attempt to enahnce those qualities.

The reliance on estimations then opens the door to the possibility that alternative means of strength testing may be necessary to truly understand if the changes in other variables were a result of strength or some other factor. In recent years, the cost of load cells has decreased, which has led to an increase in the availability of different means of utilization of load cells. This allows for more cost effective options to perform movements like the isometric midthigh pull, which is often seen as a gold standard of such for force production. There are two companies that have become extremely popular with those who test isometric midthigh pull and don't have a large budget - Vernier and Pasco. These two companies use a bend load cell to reduce the cost and maintain high quality data. They are amazingly accurate devices and quite durable for isometric testing. Durability tends to decrease when we discuss the performance of jumps on these devices. As this technology has become increasingly available for coaches, it may be necessary to talk about the use of the Dynamic Strength Index (DSI) and its use in testing for athletes. Since many practitioners are using force plates to measure isometric strength and dynamic strength, it is quite beneficial to examine their relationship to know what needs to be shifted toward strength or the utilization of more velocity.

The DSI is calculated by looking at the peak force during the concentric (or propulsive phase) of the countermovement jump and dividing it by the peak force of the isometric midthigh pull. This ratio will produce a number, typically between 0 and 1.0. Jeremy Sheppard and his group have provided some guidelines. When someone has a DSI between 0.6 and 0.8, they respond best to mixed training, so essentially remain on the same path of training that is currently being performed. If the person is greater than 0.8, this indicates that they are weak and need to focus more on maximal strength. If the number is below 0.6, this indicates that they are strong but slow and need to focus more on ballistics.

It would be nice if this index was this simple, but it never is. Context of the population and individual needs to be applied here. We all know that Bompa was correct, for a while, that increases in maximal strength will cause improvements in rate of force development, yielding strength, and far beyond. With this realization, that context needs to be applied. If individuals are unable to pull approximately 49N/kg for men and 44N/kg for females, their greatest focus needs to be on strength. The possible exception would be dealing with individuals I would consider the freaks of freaks. What I mean by this is that there are RARE individuals who come in, having never lifted weights, and are the fastest and best jumpers on the team. These individuals often don't respond well to heavy loads. These individuals are rare - there were only a handful of them who came through the program in my 20-plus years of experience. For the most part, those who come in are weak, and simply getting them strong will allow for higher performance.

When athletes are strong enough and need to improve their ballistic strength, the utilization of VBT is a fantastic first step. First implement strength-speed and continue to check their DSI. If the numbers are not improving after six weeks of performance, a higher speed movement may be necessary and the addition of accommodating resistance such as bands, chains, electric and electromagnetic motors may all be utilized quite effectively for this. Once gains with speed-strength cease, it may be necessary to utilize other special exercises to further elicit adaptations.

This of course begs the question, how do we know if the exercise had an influence? This is interesting to me, and seems to be an age-old question that everyone tends to want to ask, but then avoids rather than addressing. Zatsiorsky in his book "Science and Practice of Strength Training" addressed a tool called the "Transfer Index" back in 1995, so for a quarter of a century we have been looking for a tool that has been in a foundational text that most have read. I bring this up primarily because we need to revisit foundational texts. We frequently only see what we are ready to see, not what is in the book. The transfer index deals with result gains and will compare the two to see what the impact of one was on the other. Typically what is examined is a key performance indicator, which is untrained, and then it's compared to the exercise that was trained. Result gains are calculated as follows:

Result gain= (Post testing change score mean)÷(Pre testing standard deviation)

This allows you to make sure everything is on the same scale and removes the units from the metric to make a clean calculation. The transfer index is then calculated by dividing the two result gains, again with the key performance indicator being the numerator and trained exercise the denominator.

As an example, say we are examining the impact of squat on sprints in a college football team. If we examine the entire team and see that the pre- test of the squat had a mean of 486 pounds with a standard deviation of 181 pounds, and at post test saw an average improvement of 380 pounds with a standard deviation of 430 pounds, this would have a result gain equation of 381 pounds (mean post test change)/181lbs (pre standard deviation). The units would then cancel out and leave us with a result gain of 0.21 for the squat. If for the 40 we had a pretest mean of 4.84s and standard deviation of 1.29s, and a post test change of 0.04s and standard deviation of 0.11s, it would actually indicate that the athletes got slower for the training period. This would have a result gain equation of 0.04s/1.29s for a result gain of 0.03. We then would have the result gain of the 40 divided by the result gain of the squat, so 0.03/0.21 to give us a transfer index of 0.14.

Context must be applied to the transfer index of course. If your squat is positive, this is typically a good thing. If your sprint is negative, this would indicate that you improved in speed. In this instance we see that the sprint is positive, and the squat is positive, and we have a positive transfer index. If we had a negative squat result gain, meaning that the athlete got weaker, and a negative 40 result gain, indiciating the athlete got faster, then we would also have a positive transfer index. Another condition would be if the athlete had a negative squat result gain (got weaker) and a positive 40 result gain (got slower), then we would have a negative transfer index. So simply calculating an index isn't enough. You must understand the context of the numbers.

What is a good and bad transfer depends also on the context of the population. For instance, if you are dealing with a highly trained group of athletes and achieved a -0.2 transfer index for squat and sprint speed (with the context of an increase in squat and decrease in sprint time), this would be amazing, whereas experiencing the same score with a younger group of untrained individuals, the results may have been subpar, much to the frustration of coaches. For those of you reading this, the answers aren't cut and dried. Thus we have to look at how the numbers were derived rather than just simply say if the transfer index was good or bad.

Periodization

I think periodization is one of the most misunderstood aspects to strength & conditioning. All that periodization means is that it is the breaking up of the entire training year into periods. It is not about sets, reps, intensities, exercises, or any other single variable. Can it be that? For some sports, absolutely. If the sport is a barbell sport, then of course the SPP done in training is the sport itself, so it follows different qualifiers. For most sports, though, it is not that.

Can you break training into different phases? Absolutely. It should be done that way for one trait to potentiate the next. As the organelle of the muscle cell reorganizes in response to each session, then it only makes sense. However, does this mean that you have to do X repetitions for Y sets with Z loading and AA rest interval? No, absolutely not. In fact, I have a great appreciation for how some eastern bloc practitioners have broken the training year into just two phases for periodization - GPP and SPP (a general and specific phase). It was more of a change in exercise selection than it was for intensities, but this is of course dependent upon the sport.

Let's now get down to incorporating VBT into your typical periodization plan. There are really an infinite number of methods that are possible for this, and we will discuss only a few here.

In traditional periodization plans, there are often anatomical adaptation phases, hypertrophy phases, strength phases, and then strength/power phases. We will break down each phase briefly for its purpose and then how to incorporate velocity, or if you even should. Yes, I said if you even should.

The anatomical adaptation phase is typically performed to restore movement and muscle defficencies that occurred as a result of specificity of training for the sport. During this phase, of course, muscle balance is a priority as is range of motion. There is no point in adding velocity to this phase. The speed of the movement is irrelevant and in fact can be counterproductive to the point of the phase. Focus on the relevant range of motion and corrections. The addition of velocity will only impede the progress that can be made by this phase.

Hypertrophy is the next typical phase. With athletes who are underdeveloped and in need of additional mass, velocity is irrelevant. As previously seen in the study by Pareja-Blanco, greater overall hypertrophy was demonstrated when taking the athlete to greater fatigue levels. With these athletes, just have them train to greater levels of fatigue and control for technique. If the athlete approaches technical failure, the set is then ceased. For some athletes, an increased mass will lead to undesirable effects, such as a decrease in strength to mass ratio. When this is the case, velocity loss is extremely valuable. If the individual needs high levels of speed and power, using losses of 10 perdent up to 20 percent will lead to fatigue of primarily the fast twitch muscle fibers, and thus stimulate hypertrophy of those fibers only. Speed and power will typically increase as well as the relative measures.

Strength is the next typical phase. If the athlete does not understand how to strain yet, then of course velocity is irrelevant. They will see far better improvements from traditional means of training and engaging Henneman's size principle and myofibril adaptations. Those who are higher level athletes with relative strength of greater than 1.7x's body weight on a back squat will typically not see tremendous improvements through learning how to strain and extend time under tension. For these athletes, I would examine training strength in one of two ways - a set intensity with velocity loss of 10 to 20 percent, or replace the intensities with their load velocity relationship. This is demonstrated in Figure 29, where we replace the intensity with the corresponding velocity from their load-velocity profile.

Week	Phase	Sets/Reps	Vel 1 \\Vel 2	Intensity
1	Strength	3x6	.48m/s	80%
2	Strength	3x5	.41m/s	85%
3	Strength	5x3	.37m/s	87%
4	Strength	3x5	.45m/s	82%
5	Strength	5x3	.41m/s	85%
6	Strength	4x2	.33m/s	90%
7	Strength	5x3	.41m/s	85%
8	Strength	4x2	.32m/s	90%
9	S/P	3x2/5x3	.29m/s\\.97m/s	92/50%
10	S/P	5x3/5x3	.48m/s\\.97m/s	80/50%
11	S/P	5x3/6x2	.41m/s\\.89m/s	85/55%
12	S/P	4x2/6x2	.33m/s\\.80m/s	90/60%

Figure 29

Power is the next typical phase. This is where I feel that velocity is crucial. The feedback driving a faster velocity for the performance of the movement, leading to higher power adaptations and the correct load for the prescription, provides the practitioner with invaluable feedback for the athletes. Again, either the use of velocity loss for your previous program, or the utilization of velocity zones, would be game changers for your training program here. Speed and power adaptations occur relatively quickly and will be the most effective place to implement velocity. Expect changes to jumping ability, and sprint splits above 10m are very likely to improve.

The inseason is the period when velocity is also extremely effective. This is due to the increases in stressors from many areas that are often tough to account for (personal life, academic stress, etc). The load velocity relationship or prescription of a velocity zone here takes into account the sport and outside stressors to allow for the athlete to be training appropriately. HOWEVER, if the athlete does not possess sufficient strength or technique, don't utilize VBT. They will see far greater improvements in the sporting ability through technique refinement and progressive overload on general movements.

Conclusion

Many athletes have had great success using velocity-based training (VBT). They are better able to hone in on where they need to be for that day to help them achieve optimal results. They are able to make strength and speed gains greater than before, because they can quantify exactly where they are and exactly where they need to be. The guess work is removed.

VBT devices are like extra coaches on the floor. They tell athletes whether they are moving at a rate that calls for additional weight on the bar or whether they need to take weight off. In essence, with a well-trained group of athletes, VBT device use is like doubling or tripling the size of your coaching staff, because the unit selects the weights for you.

The methods listed in this manual have been tried and they are practical. They all work. Find what works best for you. Don't miss out on this incredible methodology because you don't know how to use the various devices.

This manual is a starting point for coaches. Get a measurement device, read this manual and try some methods with your athletes. Figure out what works. Use it, get results and help your athletes achieve their full potential. Find what works the best for your athletes, even if it is something new. Beyond that, share what you find. We could have so much more information to train athletes with if we just shared.

Epilogue

I am floored with the response I have received from this book as well as from my many articles and talks around the world. I never expected the reception to be so warm to this. I am not sure about many things in this

World, or even in velocity-based training (VBT). I am sure of one thing though - this book will continue to evolve and expand just as it has since 2008.

There are things that I have debated about putting into this text, as I have learned a lot while writing it. There's more work than ever coming out now. There's more information, more knowledge and more application. Over the years, I have changed what I have recommended greatly. As time goes on and the implementation of different devices improves, we may go in an entirely different direction in the future. What is that direction? What will it look like in 10, 20, 30 or 40 years, if I'm blessed enough to still be alive and working? I don't have any clue. There are more questions than answers, and I think that is a beautiful thing.

I do believe that we will be moving toward giving prescriptions of individual lifts and what the velocity cutoffs and progressions and relationships should be at various percentages of a 1RM. Beyond this, who knows? As my good friend Brett Bartholomew always says, "Failure is fertilizer." I have failed and found what doesn't work for many things with VBT. The ground is very fertile, and I can't wait to see what grows from here in the future.

I have had the great fortune of talking with many of the other people out in the VBT world over the past few years. Due to the flatness of the world thanks to the internet, I have been able to converse with brilliant people such as Lorena Torres-Ronda, Carl Valle, Eamonn Flanagan and Dan Baker, to name a few. While we all have disagreements on a few points, the key to everything is that we agree on way more than we disagree. Our disagreements typically lie in either small details or the way in which we apply VBT to our athletes in our groups.

References

Ajan, T., Baroga, Lazar. (1988). *Weightlifting: Fitness for All Sports* (First ed.). Budapest, Hungary: International Weightlifint Federation.

Deci, E. L., & Ryan, R. M. (2012). Self-determination theory.

Fry, A. C., Kraemer, W. J., van Borselen, F., Lynch, J. M., Marsit, J. L., Roy, E. P., . . . Knuttgen, H. G. (1994). Performance decrements with high-intensity resistance exercise overtraining. *Med Sci Sports Exerc, 26*(9), 1165-1173. Retrieved from http://www.ncbi.nlm.nih.gov/entrez/query.fcgi?cmd=Retrieve&db=PubMed&dopt=Citation&list_uids=7808252

Galpin, A. J., Malyszek, K. K., Davis, K. A., Record, S. M., Brown, L. E., Coburn, J. W., . . . Manolovitz, A. D. (2015). Acute Effects of Elastic Bands on Kinetic Characteristics During the Deadlift at Moderate and Heavy Loads. *J Strength Cond Res, 29*(12), 3271-3278. doi:10.1519/jsc.0000000000000987

Gonzalez-Badillo, J. J., Marques, M. C., & Sanchez-Medina, L. (2011). The importance of movement velocity as a measure to control resistance training intensity. *J Hum Kinet, 29A*, 15-19. doi:10.2478/v10078-011-0053-6

González-Badillo, J. J., & Sánchez-Medina, L. (2010). Movement velocity as a measure of loading intensity in resistance training. *Int J Sports Med, 31*(5), 347-352. Retrieved from http://www.scopus.com/inward/record.url?eid=2-s2.0-77951642845&partnerID=40&md5=0edc309dacdb1b84395b805178c03886

Haff, G. G., & Triplett, N. T. (2015). *Essentials of strength training and conditioning 4th edition*: Human kinetics.

Harbili, E., & Alptekin, A. (2014). Comparative kinematic analysis of the snatch lifts in elite male adolescent weightlifters. *J Sports Sci Med, 13*(2), 417-422.

Heiderscheit, B. C., Sherry, M. A., Silder, A., Chumanov, E. S., & Thelen, D. G. (2010). Hamstring strain injuries: recommendations for diagnosis, rehabilitation, and injury prevention. *Journal of Orthopaedic & Sports Physical Therapy, 40*(2), 67-81.

Helms, E. R., Storey, A., Cross, M. R., Brown, S. R., Lenetsky, S., Ramsay, H., . . . Zourdos, M. C. (2017). RPE and Velocity Relationships for the Back Squat, Bench Press, and Deadlift in Powerlifters. *The Journal of Strength & Conditioning Research, 31*(2), 292-297. doi:10.1519/jsc.0000000000001517

Jacobson, B. H., Conchola, E., Smith, D. B., Akehi, K., & Glass, R. (2014). The Relationship between Selected Strength and Power Assessments to Peak and Average Velocity of the Drive Block in Offensive Line Play. *J Strength Cond Res, Publish Ahead of Print.* doi:10.1519/JSC.0000000000000552

Jacobson, B. H., Conchola, E. G., Glass, R. G., & Thompson, B. J. (2013). Longitudinal Morphological and Performance Profiles for American, NCAA Division I Football Players. *The Journal of Strength & Conditioning Research, 27*(9), 2347-2354 2310.1519/JSC.2340b2013e31827fcc31827d. Retrieved from http://journals.lww.com/nsca-jscr/Fulltext/2013/09000/Longitudinal_Morphological_and_Performance.1.aspx

Jennings, C. L., Viljoen, W., Durandt, J., & Lambert, M. I. (2005). The reliability of the FitroDyne as a measure of muscle power. *J Strength Cond Res, 19*(4), 859-863. Retrieved from http://www.ncbi.nlm.nih.gov/entrez/query.fcgi?cmd=Retrieve&db=PubMed&dopt=Citation&list_uids=16287353

Jidovtseff, B., Quièvre, J., Hanon, C., & Crielaard, J. M. (2009). Inertial muscular profiles allow a more accurate training loads definition. *Les profils musculaires inertiels permettent une définition plus précise des charges d'entraînement, 24*(2), 91-96. Retrieved from http://www.scopus.com/inward/record.url?eid=2-s2.0-63249115161&partnerID=40&md5=e2235303ef0f6c81e8a8b0741b631260

Jimenez-Reyes, P., Samozino, P., & Morin, J.-B. (2019). Optimized training for jumping performance using the force-velocity imbalance: Individual adaptation kinetics. *PLOS ONE, 14*, e0216681. doi:10.1371/journal.pone.0216681

Jovanovic, M., Flanagan, Eamonn. (2014). Rearched Applications of Velocity Based Strength Training. *Journal of Australian Strength and Conditioning, 22*(2), 58-68.

Mann, J. B., Ivey, P. A., & Sayers, S. P. (2015). Velocity-Based Training in Football. *Strength & Conditioning Journal, 37*(6), 52-57. doi:10.1519/ssc.0000000000000177

Mann, J. B., Thyfault, J. P., Ivey, P. A., & Sayers, S. P. (2010). The effect of autoregulatory progressive resistance exercise vs. linear periodization on strength improvement in college athletes. *J Strength Cond Res, 24*(7), 1718-1723. doi:10.1519/JSC.0b013e3181def4a6

Pareja-Blanco, F., Rodriguez-Rosell, D., Sanchez-Medina, L., Sanchis-Moysi, J., Dorado, C., Mora-Custodio, R., . . . Gonzalez-Badillo, J. J. (2016). Effects of velocity loss during resistance training on athletic performance, strength gains and muscle adaptations. *Scand J Med Sci Sports.* doi:10.1111/sms.12678

Randell, A. D., Cronin, J. B., Keogh, J. W., Gill, N. D., & Pedersen, M. C. (2011). Effect of instantaneous performance feedback during 6 weeks of velocity-based resistance training on sport-specific performance tests. *J Strength Cond Res, 25*(1), 87-93. doi:10.1519/JSC.0b013e3181fee634

Roman, R. A. (1986). *The Training of the Weightlifter* (A. Charniga, Trans. 1 ed.). Moscow: Sportivny Press.

Sanchez-Medina, L., & Gonzalez-Badillo, J. J. (2011). Velocity loss as an indicator of neuromuscular fatigue during resistance training. *Med Sci Sports Exerc, 43*(9), 1725-1734. doi:10.1249/MSS.0b013e318213f880

Serrano, N., Colenso-Semple, L. M., Lazauskus, K. K., Siu, J. W., Bagley, J. R., Lockie, R. G., . . . Galpin, A. J. (2019). Extraordinary fast-twitch fiber abundance in elite weightlifters. *PLOS ONE, 14*(3), e0207975-e0207975. doi:10.1371/journal.pone.0207975

Siff, M. C. (2000). *Supertraining* (5th ed.). Denver, Co.

Simmons, L. (2002). Measuring Speed: The Tendo Unit. *PowerliftingUSA.*

Simmons, L. (2007). *The Westside Barbell Book of Methods* (1st ed.). Grove City, OH: Action Printing.

Suchomel, T. J., Comfort, P., & Stone, M. H. (2015). Weightlifting Pulling Derivatives: Rationale for Implementation and Application. *Sports Medicine, 45*(6), 823-839. doi:10.1007/s40279-015-0314-y

Suchomel, T. J., Nimphius, S., & Stone, M. H. (2016). The Importance of Muscular Strength in Athletic Performance. *Sports Med, 46*(10), 1419-1449. doi:10.1007/s40279-016-0486-0

Trappe, S., Luden, N., Minchev, K., Raue, U., Jemiolo, B., & Trappe, T. A. (2015). Skeletal muscle signature of a champion sprint runner. *J Appl Physiol (1985), 118*(12), 1460-1466. doi:10.1152/japplphysiol.00037.2015

Wallace, B. J., Winchester, J. B., & McGuigan, M. R. (2006). Effects of elastic bands on force and power characteristics during the back squat exercise. *J Strength Cond Res, 20*(2), 268-272. doi:10.1519/r-16854.1

Weakley, J., McLaren, S., Ramirez-Lopez, C., Garcia-Ramos, A., Dalton-Barron, N., Banyard, H., . . . Jones, B. (2019). Application of velocity loss thresholds during free-weight resistance training: Responses and reproducibility of perceptual, metabolic, and neuromuscular outcomes. *J Sports Sci*, 1-9. doi:10.1080/02640414.2019.1706831

Zatsiorsky, V. M. (1995). *Science and Practice of Strength Training*. Champaign, IL: Human Kinetics.

Acknowledgements

First, I would like to thank my wife, Corinne, for putting up with me, my crazy career, my hair-brained ideas and the long hours spent away from home visiting other places. Next, I would like to thank the department of athletics from the University of Miami for allowing me to be a part of their program. I would like to thank Rick Perry, Pat Ivey, Joe Kenn, Tom Myslinski and Buddy Morris for being such great mentors to me and for allowing a young strength coach to follow Mylo and Buddy into a bar and pull out pen and paper at the table without kicking him out.

Maybe this one holds the key to the future of VBT—my daughter on her first trip to the gym. What's the first thing she went for? The GymAware. I couldn't be prouder.

I would like to thank Louie Simmons for introducing the VBT concepts and the Tendo to this country and for being open about sharing his knowledge and methods with anyone and everyone. Love him or hate him, he's been a great contributor to the strength game in the United States. No matter who's lifting, as long as Louie Simmons is at Westside Barbell, they will always be cutting edge.

To all of the rest of you out there who have influenced me on my journey, there are too many to mention, so thank you.

About the Author

Dr. Bryan Mann is currently an assitant professor of Kinesiology and Sports Sciences at the University of Miami and can be reached via email at jbryanmann@gmail.com or social media @jbryanmann.

What People Are Saying About VBT and Its Techniques

"Dr. Mann's velocity-based training allows me to train right where I need to be each and every week. I feel that the velocity feedback is another coach telling me when to go up and down, not only each week but each set, as well as when to stop. It's been a very valuable tool for me."

—Christian Cantwell

Shot-putter, 6-time world champion 2008 Olympics Silver Medalist

"Dr. Mann's work has had a huge impact in the development of our athletes. The ability to continually monitor the athletes' outputs to prescribe the proper intensities throughout the year has allowed our athletes to continually develop through their later years in college. I couldn't recommend his work and this resource enough."

— Jay DeMayo

University of Richmond

"Velocity-based training makes sure that my athletes are training where they need to be for that day. It gives instant feedback and contributes to a competitive environment for my athletes. No one wants to be outdone. It has been an invaluable and integral part of our training."

—David Deets

Director of Basketball Strength and Conditioning, University of Tulsa

"For so many years, strength coaches were frustrated because we understood that if a weight was lifted with speed, we could develop athletes to a higher level. Many coaches came up with some great ideas, but we needed some method of measuring the speed that the bar moved. Then came the Tendo unit, and now we are able to give our athletes instant feedback on how fast the bar moves. We are able to develop strength through speed of movement—the type of speed-strength that we need for our athletes on the field. Using velocity also encourages competition between athletes, which elevates their abilities and our team's success. Our team has not only maintained our strength but has been able to increase our strength during the season for the past three years due to using velocity. Our new personal records are at an average of 85 percent in our post-season records compared to our pre-season testing, and it's because of training off of velocity during our in-season workouts. Also, during that same time, we have not lost a football game in November because while everyone else is trying to maintain we are getting stronger."

—Bill Gillespie

Director of Strength and Conditioning, Liberty University

Bench press specialist

"Developing Explosive Athletes was a Game Changer for me. I can honestly say, very few books have had the type of impact on the programs I write for our athletes, than this book has. Dr. Bryan Mann is a in the trenches practitioner, that has the unique ability to take the complex and make simple. He and his work is an incredible resource for coaches and athletes alike."

— Ron McKeefery, MA, RSCC*E, MSCC

Fresno State University 2x Collegiate S&C of the Year

Printed in Germany
by Amazon Distribution
GmbH, Leipzig